saints and sanctity

PRENTICE-HALL INTERNATIONAL, INC., *London*
PRENTICE-HALL OF AUSTRALIA, PTY., LTD., *Sydney*
PRENTICE-HALL OF CANADA, LTD., *Toronto*
PRENTICE-HALL OF INDIA (PRIVATE) LTD., *New Delhi*
PRENTICE-HALL OF JAPAN, INC., *Tokyo*

saints and sanctity
walter j. burghardt, s. j.

Prentice-Hall, Inc., Englewood Cliffs, N.J.

Imprimi potest   John M. Daley, S.J.
                  Provincial, Maryland Province, Society of Jesus

Nihil obstat   Carroll E. Satterfield
                  Censor, Archdiocese of Baltimore

Imprimatur ✠   Lawrence Cardinal Shehan
                  Archbishop of Baltimore

                  July 19, 1965

The *nihil obstat* and *imprimatur* are official decla-
rations that a book or pamphlet is free of doctrinal
or moral error. No implication is contained therein
that those who have granted the *nihil obstat* and
imprimatur agree with the opinions expressed.

Illustrations of the saints by Jordan Myers.

preface

Saints and Sanctity was born slowly of a problem—a problem in contemporary spirituality. What is the significance of yesterday's saint for today's Christian? What meaning has the sanctity of the past for the holiness of the present?

On broad lines, three solutions may be suggested—two extremes (I do not use the word disparagingly) and a middle. One extreme insists that usually the lives of the saints are normative for us: what they did, we must do. This imitation the Church herself would seem to recommend in her official prayers, in the Mass and breviary. We are to "imitate what we revere" in the protomartyr Stephen, his spirit of forgiveness; we are to "follow continually the faith" of the apostle Thomas, "imitate the actions" of Paul the first hermit, "follow" Agnes of Rome "by our virtuous way of life," "follow avidly the advice and example" of Peter Damiani. And so on, unceasingly.

What we revere in the saints, this we ought imitate.

The other extreme affirms that the lives of the saints have little or nothing to say to contemporary man. These men and women lived, for the most part, in ages unlike our own. The situations in which they achieved sanctity are never quite repeated today. Their experiences and inner dynamisms are not reflected in our own. Read the lives of the saints, from John the Baptist and Ignatius of Antioch through Patrick and Boniface to Martin de Porres and Teresa of Lisieux, and you find yourself in other worlds—fascinating history, of course, and often impressively heroic, but too different from the modern age to be genuinely relevant. Revere the saints, yes: imitate them, no.

The position, or presupposition, that underlies this book is in the nature of a *via media*, an effort to harmonize and unify the valid insights of both extremes. In this approach, the saints do have something precious to say to us, but their appeal is not to slavish imitation. In other words, the details that dot their lives may well be outmoded, dictated by ephemeral circumstances. Antony the Hermit locking himself in an Egyptian tomb; Martin de Porres asking his superior to sell him into slavery; Patrick praying on a snowcapped mountain; Aquinas casting his theology in song; Canisius hammering away relentlessly at heresy; Xavier dying alone six miles from China; the Good Thief crucified an arm's length from Christ; Agnes leaving life at twelve or thirteen; all those saints who never bathed, refused to lift their eyes, slept rarely, ate reluctantly— it is not this that calls for imitation. Even when the finger of God is clearly there, these are individual actions, personal manifestations of inner drives, historically conditioned expressions of faith and love.

But even in these highly personalized actions the saints do speak to us. The point that this book makes is that the lives of the saints, or aspects of their lives, or individual episodes in their lives, even legends surrounding saints who did or did not exist—these illustrate in striking fashion certain principles or facets of Christian spirituality that are permanently valid, that have a relevance transcending persons and places, eras and situations. And even where saintly actions seem embarrassingly eccentric or bizarre, they often lend credence to Chesterton's contention: "A saint is one who exaggerates what the world and the Church have forgotten."

Saints and Sanctity does not try to

prove this thesis. It is not proof that each chapter offers, but witness. I have found the connection between these figures of the past and the needs of the present uncommonly compelling. I can only hope that readers of the following pages will enjoy a similar experience, will capture to some extent the ageless wisdom that lies hidden in the pages of the past.

With one exception, the chapters of this book were originally written for oral delivery. In many instances I have modified, at times rather drastically, the original content: the passage of time, fresh insights, new situations with new needs, the suggestions of several gracious critics—all have combined to give new life to older materials. The basic structure of each chapter, however, remains what it was; occasionally, even the audience (students, doctors, convicts) comes into view.

The chapters on Ignatius of Antioch, Antony, Athanasius, Augustine, and Jerome were delivered as radio addresses on the "Catholic Hour" in 1959 on the general theme "The Catholic Concept of Sanctity," with the saints chosen from my specialized field of research, the Fathers of the Church. The chapters on Patrick, Francis Xavier, Agnes, and Mary Magdalene continued that general theme over the "Catholic Hour" in 1964, without being restricted to the patristic era. The chapter on Thomas Aquinas was delivered on CBS's "Church of the Air" in 1962. The chapter on Peter Canisius was a convocation address to the faculty and students of Canisius College, Buffalo, N.Y., in April of 1955. The chapter on Christopher was preached at the annual Mass of the St. Mary's Deanery of the Archdiocesan Council of Catholic Women, Leonardtown, Md., in April of 1960. The chapter on Luke was addressed to the students and faculty of the Georgetown University Medical School, Washington, D.C., during the annual Votive Mass of St. Luke, in October of 1959. The chapter on Dismas is a conflation of two sermons delivered to the inmates of the Maryland Penitentiary, Baltimore, Md., on the occasion of the Votive Mass of St. Dismas, in October of 1958, and October of 1964. The chapter on Monica was given at the Communion Breakfast of the Mothers' Club of Loyola High School, Towson, Md., in January of 1962. The chapters on Andrew, Nicholas, Lucy, and Thomas the Apostle were originally a series of four sermons on the "Advent saints" preached in St. Ignatius Loyola Church, New York City, in Advent of 1959. The chapter on Martin de Porres was written specifically for this book, because it seemed to be demanded by the color crisis of our time.

WALTER J. BURGHARDT, S.J.

acknowledgments

The author wishes to acknowledge permission to reprint material from the following:

Ancient Christian Writers, Vol 1 and 17 (Westminster, Md.: The Newman Press, 1946). Reprinted by permission of the publishers.

James Brodrick, S.J., *Saint Peter Canisius* (Chicago: Loyola University Press, 1962). Reprinted by permission of the publishers.

Sister Mary Ignatius, "Discovery," *Messenger of the Sacred Heart,* Vol. 77, No. 2 (Feb., 1942). Reprinted by permission of the publishers.

The poem, "Saint for Our Time," is reprinted from *The Unicorn and Other Poems* by Anne Morrow Lindbergh by permission of Random House, Inc. © copyright 1956 by Anne Morrow Lindbergh.

F. J. Sheed, trans., *Confessions of St. Augustine* (New York: Sheed & Ward, Inc., 1943). Reprinted by permission of the publishers.

The author also wishes to express his gratitude for the following articles of his, which have previously appeared in other publications:

"St. Agnes," "St. Francis Xavier," "St. Patrick," and "St. Mary Magdalene," radio addresses delivered on "Catholic Hour" (March, 1964). Reprinted and adapted by permission of the National Council of Catholic Men in cooperation with the National Broadcasting Company.

ACKNOWLEDGMENTS

"St. Ignatius of Antioch," "St. Antony the Hermit," "St. Athanasius," "St. Augustine," and "St. Jerome," radio addresses delivered on "Catholic Hour" (May, 1959). Reprinted and adapted by permission of the National Council of Catholic Men in cooperation with the National Broadcasting Company.

"The Beloved Physician: St. Luke," *The Georgetown Medical Bulletin*, Vol. 13, No. 3 (Feb., 1960). Reprinted and adapted by permission of the publishers.

"Sanctity and Intelligence," radio address delivered on "Catholic Hour" (May 13, 1962) and subsequently printed in *Catholic Mind*, Vol. 60, No. 1167 (Nov., 1962). Reprinted by permission of the National Council of Catholic Men in cooperation with the Columbia Broadcasting System and also by permission of *Catholic Mind*, The Monthly Review of Christian Thought and Documentation, 106 W. 56th Street, New York, N.Y. 10019.

"The Vision of Peter Canisius," *Catholic Mind*, Vol. 55, No. 1129 (Feb., 1957). Reprinted by permission of *Catholic Mind*, The Monthly Review of Christian Thought and Documentation, 106 W. 56th Street, New York, N.Y. 10019.

contents

ST. IGNATIUS OF ANTIOCH

SANCTITY AND MARTYRDOM   1

ST. ANTONY THE HERMIT

SANCTITY AND SOLITUDE   13

ST. ATHANASIUS

SANCTITY AND ACTIVITY   25

ST. AUGUSTINE

SANCTITY AND CONVERSION   37

ST. JEROME

SANCTITY AND PASSION   49

ST. MARTIN DE PORRES

SANCTITY AND COLOR   61

ST. PATRICK

SANCTITY AND ANCESTRY   75

ST. THOMAS AQUINAS

SANCTITY AND INTELLIGENCE   87

ST. PETER CANISIUS

SANCTITY AND EDUCATION   101

xiii

ST. CHRISTOPHER
SANCTITY AND SELFLESSNESS   117

ST. LUKE
SANCTITY AND MEDICINE   129

ST. FRANCIS XAVIER
SANCTITY AND FRUSTRATION   141

ST. DISMAS
SANCTITY AND CAPTIVITY   153

ST. MONICA
SANCTITY AND MOTHERHOOD   167

ST. AGNES
SANCTITY AND AGE   179

ST. ANDREW
SANCTITY AND THE SEARCH
FOR CHRIST   191

ST. NICHOLAS
SANCTITY AND THE CHRISTMAS
GIFT   201

ST. LUCY
SANCTITY AND LIGHT   209

ST. THOMAS THE APOSTLE
SANCTITY AND CHRISTMAS FAITH   217

ST. MARY MAGDALENE
SANCTITY AND EASTER RENEWAL   227

saints and sanctity

st. ignatius of antioch

sanctity and martyrdom

IT WAS about the year 110. In Antioch of Syria, persecution racked the Christian Church. And the Bishop of Antioch, Ignatius, was cast in chains. Flanked by ten guards, he was dragged over land and sea to Rome, to die in the Colosseum. During that journey Ignatius managed to write seven letters—letters which have been termed the most beautiful pearls of ancient Christian literature. What grips Ignatius is a passionate love for his crucified Lord, a love so overpowering that it breaks through grammar; language is inadequate, and his ideas tumble headlong one upon the other. One letter, more than any other, has captured the imagination of the ages. He is writing to the Christians who will soon see him, the Christians of Rome. He longs to see them, to embrace them; but he is afraid—afraid,

1

he says, of their love; their love may
destroy him. Their influence with civil
authority may save him; and he does
not want that. And so he writes perhaps the most moving passage in early
Christian literature:

"I am writing to all the Churches and
state emphatically to all that I die
willingly for God, provided you do not
interfere. I beg you, do not show me
unseasonable kindness. Suffer me to be
the food of wild beasts, which are the
means of my making my way to God.
God's wheat I am, and by the teeth of
wild beasts I am to be ground that I
may prove Christ's pure bread. Better
still, coax the wild beasts to become my
tomb and to leave no part of my person behind. . . . Then only shall I be
a genuine disciple of Jesus Christ when
the world will not see even my body.
Petition Christ in my behalf that through
these instruments I may prove God's
sacrifice. . . . Oh, may the beasts prepared for me be my joy! And I pray
that they may be found to be ready
for me. I will even coax them to make
short work of me, not as has happened
to some whom they were too timid to
touch. And should they be unwilling to
attack me who am willing, I will myself
compel them. . . . May nothing seen or
unseen fascinate me, so that I may

2

happily make my way to Jesus Christ! Fire, cross, struggles with wild beasts, wrenching of bones, mangling of limbs, crunching of the whole body, cruel tortures inflicted by the devil—let them come upon me, provided only I make my way to Jesus Christ.

"Of no use to me will be the farthest reaches of the universe or the kingdoms of this world. I would rather die and come to Jesus Christ than be king over the entire earth. Him I seek who died for us; Him I love who rose again because of us. . . . Do not make a gift to the world of one who wants to be God's. . . . Permit me to be an imitator of my suffering God. If anyone holds Him in his heart, let him understand what I am aspiring to; and then let him sympathize with me, knowing in what distress I am." [1]

Not long after, Ignatius, Bishop of Antioch, died by the teeth of wild beasts in the Roman Colosseum.

For many a critic, Ignatius of Antioch is a fanatic. Less than fifteen years ago a prolific author wrote of him: This "strange saint, wandering slowly toward Rome, left his mark on Christianity. All

---

[1] Ignatius of Antioch, *Letter to the Romans* 4-6; trans. James A. Kleist, S.J., in *Ancient Christian Writers* 1 (Westminster, Md.: Newman Press, 1946), 81-83.

3

the wilder elements descend from him, from the terrible look in his eyes." [2] From this point of view, Ignatius is Christianity at its worst, sanctity at its most repugnant. This lust for martyrdom is a neurotic thing. This thirst for fire and cross and wild beasts is unnatural. It is a weakling's flight from reality. Death is his love—not life. How utterly different from another Ignatius fourteen centuries later! Ignatius of Loyola is speaking to one of his first companions, James Lainez:

Ignatius: Tell me, Master Lainez, what do you think you would do, were God our Lord to say: "If you want to die soon, I will release you from the prison of this body and give you eternal glory. If you prefer to stay alive, I give you no assurance as to what will become of you. . . ." If our Lord told you this, and you thought that by remaining for some time in this life you could render some outstanding service to His Divine Majesty, which would you choose?

Lainez: I must confess, Father, I would choose to go soon to enjoy God and to assure my salvation and to avoid the perils in so important a matter.

Ignatius: I certainly would not. If I thought that by remaining in this life I could render some signal service to our Lord, I would beg Him to leave me here until

[2] Robert Payne, *The Fathers of the Western Church* (New York: Viking Press, 1951), p. 30.

4

I had done it; and I would not think twice of the peril to me or the assurance of my salvation.[3]

This attitude, says the critic, is Christian humanism: to serve men, not to save me. This is Christian heroism: to risk not fire and sword, but hell itself. This is Christian realism: to lust for life, not for death.

In point of fact, the criticism is unchristian. In the Christian scheme of things, martyrdom is, first, a valid way to God, to personal sanctity; it is, second, a unique witness to Christian truth; it is, third, a source of sanctification for others.

In the first place, martyrdom is a valid way to God, to personal sanctity. Sanctity, at its simplest and most profound, is union, oneness, with God. That is why God fashioned man from the dust of the earth; that is why God refashioned man from the wood of the cross: so that man and God might be one, that a creature of flesh and blood might share God's life and God's love. This oneness, this marvelous marriage of the human and the divine, this life of love, has its beginning now: "If anyone love me," the Son of God revealed at the Last

[3] Pedro de Rivadeneira, *Vida del bienaventurado Padre Ignacio de Loyola,* 2nd ed. (Barcelona: Subirana, 1885), pp. 501-2.

Supper, "my Father will love him, and we will come to him and make our home with him" (Jn 14:23). But this is only love's beginning, only the birth of union. Man's life of love, man's oneness with God, finds its consummation at death: "For those who believe," each Mass for the Dead insists, "life is not taken away, life is merely changed." It is through death that faith gives way to vision, hope is swallowed up in possession, lover grasps Beloved in eternal ecstasy. For this the Christian lives; for this he dies.

Martyrdom is one way to that endless oneness. So true is this that, in the eyes of the Church, the blood of a martyr, like the water of baptism, removes all sin, all punishment for sin, all that can delay heaven. There is no greater love, Christ assures me, than to lay down my life for my friends; then surely there is no greater love than to lay down my life for my God. If this is fanaticism, then the first Christian fanatic was Christ. For martyrdom is imitation of Christ in the most significant act of His life, the sacrifice of Himself, a sacrifice that is born of love and looks to union as the fruit of love. A martyr like Ignatius is not simply giving his body to beasts; he is giving all that he is to God. And he does it gladly; not always without fear, but always without regret. Not to

escape reality, but to face Reality—to face, in unending vision, the most real of all beings. This is Christian realism.

In the second place, martyrdom is a unique witness to Christian truth. Every Christian is a witness. For every baptism is a mission: to share Christ's role of prophet, the task of announcing the gospel, the good news that in the flesh of Christ salvation is come. Such is the task of the Body of Christ; such is the task of each member of the Body. Each Christian can proclaim with Christ: "This is why *I* was born, this is why *I* have come into the world: to bear witness to the truth" (Jn 18:37). In this way his personal sanctity, his oneness with God, bursts the bonds of his isolated self and proclaims to the world the Christ who hides in his soul.

But Christian witness is a many-splendored thing. Aquinas bears witness with his pen and Chrysostom from the pulpit; the Curé of Ars in the confessional and Teresa in Carmel; Antony in the desert, Athanasius in exile, and Xavier on the missions; Leo from the Chair of Peter, and Philip Neri on the streets of Rome. And Ignatius of Antioch —Ignatius bears witness in the Colosseum. Supreme witness, unexampled, unparalleled; for it means that the faith he carried in his heart, the faith which fell from his lips and flowed from his pen, this faith he sealed gladly with his blood. Greater witness than this no man can give. Our very language confesses it; for the first-century Christians took the word "martyr"—anyone who bears witness—and they made it mean for all ages one who dies for his witness, one who witnesses unto death the faith that is in him. For them, the first martyrdom took place on Calvary; for us, ever since Calvary the supreme witness is death. And so St. Peter writes: "Christ suffered for you, leaving you an example: you were to follow in His steps" (1 Pt 2:21). And so Ignatius begs: "Permit me to be an imitator of my suffering God." This is Christian heroism.

In the third place, martyrdom is a source of sanctification for others. Here again the model is Christ. "Unless the grain of wheat fall into the ground and die, it remains alone. But if it die, it brings forth much fruit" (Jn 12:24-25). In Catholic theology, Calvary is not simply inspiration, not simply history's prime example of the lengths to which love is willing to go. Calvary is love's finest hour because it *did* something: death won life; God's death won God's life for man.

Similarly for Ignatius, for every Christian martyr. Martyrdom has no value,

9

makes no sense, apart from Christ's cross.
But united with the Sacrifice that redeemed a world, the sacrifice of an
Ignatius brings God's life to individual
souls. The martyr is not selfish; the
Church knows no martyrs who have
loved only God and not their fellow men.
"My love for you," Ignatius writes to a
Christian community on his way to
death, "my love for you overflows all
bounds." [4] In the Colosseum, as on
Calvary, "the good shepherd lays down
his life *for his sheep*" (Jn 10:11)—not
merely in their stead, to save them from
a similar fate, but for their sanctification, so that grace, a little more of God's
life, may thrill through the Christian
body. "The blood of Christians is seed" [5]
indeed: it produces other Christians, and
it produces better Christians. Greater
love than this no man has. This is Christian humanism.

It is perilous to contrast Ignatius of
Antioch with Ignatius of Loyola—for
one basic reason: the Spanish Ignatius
had a remarkable devotion to the Syrian.
In honor of the martyr, he changed his
name from Inigo to Ignatius. The first
of his maxims was a phrase from the
first Ignatius: "My Love has been cruci-

[4] *Letter to the Philadelphians* 5, 1; tr. ACW 1,
86.
[5] Tertullian, *Apology* 50, 13.

fied." [6] He made the motto of his Jesuit Order the first three letters (IHS) of the name of Jesus in Greek, because he had read in *The Golden Legend* that when the Romans tore out the heart of the martyred Ignatius, they found those letters graven on his heart in gold.

There is no contradiction between the two—only facets of sanctity. It is always God who takes the initiative, it is always God who calls. He called both saints to Rome: one He chained in a Colosseum, the other to a desk. In both places high holiness is possible; from both high holiness emerged. And still the words of our Lord remain true: greater love, whether for God or for man, greater love there cannot be than the love which lays down life itself in witness of love. This, more than anything else, is Christian realism; this is Christian heroism; this is Christian humanism.

[6] *Letter to the Romans* 7, 2; tr. ACW 1, 83.

st. antony the hermit
sanctity and solitude

ONE OF THE fascinating figures of early Christianity is an Egyptian named Antony. His parents were Christian and well-to-do, but they died when he was eighteen or twenty. Six months later Antony walked into a church and listened to a Gospel. He listened as our Lord counseled a rich young man: "If you want to be perfect, go sell all you have, give it to the poor, and come follow me" (Mt 19:21). Home Antony went, and lavished two hundred fertile acres on his townsmen; all else he sold, gave the proceeds to the poor, kept back only a small sum for his sister. Even this he gave away when he heard another Gospel: "Be not anxious for tomorrow" (Mt 6:34).

From that moment a single ideal absorbed Antony: to be alone. Through eighty-five years four retreats hid him from human eyes. First he lived just a

13

little apart from his home: he prayed, he fasted, he worked with his hands, he fought flesh and devil, he copied the virtues of saintly men about him. But this was asceticism, not solitude; so Antony fled a fair distance from home. Locked in an empty tomb, he would see no one but a friend who brought him bread at long intervals. At thirty-five he retired still further—this time an abandoned fort fifty miles south of Memphis, on the right bank of the Nile; and here he sought his solitude for twenty years. But others yearned to imitate him; they broke down his door, removed it; would-be monks peopled the mountains, their cells dotted the desert; and to them all Antony had to be father and guide. And still he longed to be alone; one final time he fled—this time to the open desert a hundred miles from Cairo, twenty miles from the Red Sea. And still the world beat a path to his desert door; the sick and the heartsore, the wealthy and the beggared, philosopher and soldier and monk, all stormed his solitude.

Antony's search ceased in 356, when he was 105: two monks buried his body in the desert, where he hoped against hope that no one would ever find it.

Such, briefly, is the story of Antony the Hermit. Ever since Antony, thou-

14

sands upon thousands of men and women have fled the city for the silent life. At this moment, in the United States, there are scores of monasteries and convents where human beings live together but have little to do with one another, little or nothing to do with the outside world. There is much more organization, much more law and obedience, than in Antony's Egypt, but the ideal is much the same. Sixty-one American cities and towns house hundreds of Discalced Carmelite nuns whom their neighbors will never see. Twelve American states hide over a thousand Trappist monks whose external life has been described by one of their number, Thomas Merton, in these harsh terms:

"The Trappist day remains, on the whole, an arduous one with plenty of hard work and long hours in choir. The monastic setting is one of great simplicity and poverty, in which little thought is given to bodily comfort. The monks are bound by a rule of strict silence. They never converse with one another, and speak only to their Superiors and then only when necessary. They rarely leave the monastery, and sometimes spend years or indeed a whole lifetime without ever seeing the nearest small town. Newspapers and radios are unknown inside the monastery, and only sparse fragments of the world's news reach the ears of the monks." [1]

There is all this in America, and much more. And the numbers are growing. In the light of this fact, a genuine problem confronts the twentieth-century man, a problem which baffles not only the pagan but many a Christian: To what purpose this quest for solitude? Is not the whole monastic manner of life unnatural? To be a monk is to be alone. But man is by nature social, not a hermit: he is fashioned by God to live not only in the *presence* of other men but in their *company*. This is especially true in our century, when modern technology has demonstrated by deeds that men are frighteningly dependent one upon another, that no man can be an island. Civilization itself is engaged in a perilous struggle for survival, and the monk dares to write: "The Monastic Church is the one who flees to a special place prepared for her by God in the wilderness, and hides her face in the Mystery of the divine silence, and prays while the great battle is being fought between earth and heaven." [2]

The problem, put very simply, is . . . sanctity and solitude. I shall grapple

[1] Thomas Merton, *The Silent Life* (New York: Farrar, Straus and Giroux, Inc., 1957), pp. 120-21.
[2] *Ibid.*, p. xiv.

with the problem in three stages, which are, in substance, the three points I made when I wrote of Ignatius, of sanctity and martyrdom. In the Christian scheme of things, the silent life, solitude, is, first, a valid way to God, to personal sanctity; it is, second, a unique witness to Christian truth; it is, third, a source of sanctification for others.

In the first place, the silent life is a valid way to God, to personal sanctity. Basically, Antony the Hermit was gripped by the realization that sanctity is union, *oneness with God.* In this realization, of course, he is not unique: every intelligent Christian is aware of that. But Antony determined that he would be one with God in *mind and will.* Even here he is not unique: every Christian who is linked to his Lord is linked to Him in mind and will. But Antony's mind was fixed on God in *contemplation:* concentration on God, on the image of God that is every man, on the reflection of God that is all creation, would lead him to a living love that is a foretaste of eternal love. Here too he is not unique: every member of a religious order, every human being consecrated to God by vow, is by profession a contemplative. No matter how active, he must be "a contemplative in action": his apostolate with men is rooted in, and

17

nourished by, his conversation with God. But an Antony is a contemplative in *solitude:* to gaze on God in love is his all. If he tears his flesh and starves his hunger, it is to put down the body's rebellion against the spirit, to unite the whole man in unwearied contemplation. If he sweats in field or forest, it is with a twin motive: to preserve his self-sufficiency, his independence, his isolation, and to build up a healthy, integrated personality—all with a view to more intense contemplation. If he paints a fresco or writes about God, his art or his theology is itself a contemplation. His very worship—divine office and daily Mass—is an effort to share consciously and intelligently in the Mystery of Christ: mind bent low in adoration.

For all this, man must be alone. Contemplation demands solitude. Anne Morrow Lindbergh phrased it splendidly in her captivating meditation, *Gift from the Sea:* "Actually these are among the most important times in one's life—when one is alone. Certain springs are tapped only when we are alone. The artist knows he must be alone to create; the writer, to work out his thoughts; the musician, to compose; the saint, to pray." [3] Yes, an Antony knows that to

[3] Anne Morrow Lindbergh, *Gift from the Sea* (New York: Pantheon Books, Inc., 1955), p. 50.

19

contemplate, he must be alone; to contemplate continuously, he must be lastingly alone.

So then: for the Antony of yesterday and for the Trappist of today, the silent life is an instrument; it is a means, not an end. Of itself, silence is no more precious in God's eyes than speech. But silence which frees the soul for conversation with God—this is splendidly Christian. In a word, solitude is a garden where contemplation may grow. And contemplation is man caught up in God. Solitude is a way to sanctity.

In the second place, the silent life is a unique witness to Christian truth, to Christ. In the early days of the Church an interesting development took place. Through the years of bitter persecution the most obvious witness to Christianity was the martyr. Ignatius and Agnes in Rome, Polycarp in Smyrna, Cyprian and Perpetua in Carthage, these and a host of others formed the pattern of Christian perfection. It was the martyr who was the perfect imitator of Christ, the genuine disciple; martyrdom was the palpable proof of love. But as persecution slackened, martyrdom of blood became a specialized vocation reserved for a few. In the search for perfection, the emphasis shifted from a sacrifice of life to a life of sacrifice, a spiritual, day-today martyrdom where a man renounced not life but the world, where he fought not beasts but the flesh, where he defied not an emperor but the devil. This was now the obvious witness to Christ; and the purest type of such witness was the monk. The Colosseum had given way to the desert, Ignatius to Antony. Each in his own way had offered God a total gift of himself, a perfect act of love.

The silent life is a singular witness to Christ, because it is at once a protest and an affirmation. It is a protest against "the world." Not against man, not against matter, but against the world in the sense of St. John: civilized life in the measure that it is a city of sin, the kingdom of the devil, hostile to God, inhuman. Antony bruising his body in Egypt's desert is a harsh protest against today's cult of comfort. The Trappist in the silence of Kentucky's Gethsemani is an eloquent protest against the cult of distraction, the organized noise that drowns out God. The Carthusian alone in his Vermont cell is a ceaseless protest against the cult of companionship, man's utter reliance on man, human love divorced from the divine.

But monastic life is an affirmation too. It is a reminder that one thing only is indispensable: oneness with God. Walk into a Carthusian cemetery; study each

21

anonymous grave, each unmarked cross; and all you can say—all you need say— is: "This man loved God."

My third point: the silent life, the way of Antony, is a source of sanctification for others. First, by example—because the monk in his solitude is so striking a witness to Christ. His very existence is a goad to easy consciences; a challenge to habit, to routine, to accepted ways of doing things; a constant reminder that every man needs some solitude, needs to be alone, if his spirit is not to dry up, if he is to have always something to give, if he is to be unbrokenly one with God.

Second, by contemplation—because the monk in his oneness with God, in his prayer and worship, profoundly affects the world he has fled. The great battles of today are not simply economic, political, technological; the weapons are not merely diplomacy, rockets, foreign aid. In the very midst of cold wars and hot, a still more significant warfare is being waged at the interior of each man's soul. Call it what you will: the struggle between God and Satan, between the City of God and the City of Man; it is basically each man's encounter with good and evil. And in this struggle—if the Christian thesis has any validity— the good man is a power for good; sanctity sanctifies; because of him, God's grace thrills through the world of men, through us. If this is true of every Christian who is one with his Lord, it is doubly true of the Christian whose gaze is fixed on Christ without wavering, whose arms are raised to Christ without wearying, in the silence and solitude of God.

Unnatural? I suspect that Antony in his desert, the Carmelite behind her grille, and the Cistercian in his cloister would be the first to confess that their life is not quite natural—though they might suggest that civilized life in today's city is not quite natural either. The life of consecrated solitude is not for every man; it is God who calls. And as it cannot be lived on sheerly human love, so it cannot be judged by sheerly human reason. This does not mean that man must stand forever mute before a baffling mystery. It does, however, invite man, in the words of Christ, to "come apart into a desert place and rest a while" (Mk 6:31). That much, at least, is for every man: to be alone with Christ for *a while*. Alone with Him, you will begin to understand that Christian solitude is not so much the absence of men as the presence of God. Eyes fixed on Him, you will begin to experience how a loving contemplation can link a soul to God. Your oneness with God, your

awareness of His presence, will be a
soundless protest against a culture with
so little time for God. And contemplation
and protest both may profoundly affect
the small world, the little acre, God
has given you to transform. Sanctity will
sanctify.

st. athanasius
sanctity and activity

O NE OF THE thrilling proverbs of history is: "Athanasius against the world." The proverb sums up a man of action and the age that provoked it. The man was an Egyptian bishop, and his age was the fourth-century world St. Jerome described when he wrote: "The whole world groaned . . . to find itself Arian." For forty-five years this small man, whom enemies called a dwarf, was Primate of Alexandria, and for most of that half-century the Christian world was crucified by a single unorthodox sentence, the slogan of a priest named Arius: "Once the Son of God did not exist."

Around that sentence the activity of Athanasius centered. For half a century he assailed it. For half a century he trumpeted to the Roman Empire that the Son of God is eternal, as God the Father is eternal; genuinely God, not by courtesy or poetry, but God as the Father is God. For that faith he lived, for it he suffered, for it he was ready to die.

In fact, the life of Athanasius reads like a modern thriller. For his faith, he defied emperors—from the Christian-minded Constantine through Julian the Apostate to the Arian Valens. He had to cope with palace intrigue, the un-happy wedding of politics and theology. He faced the drawn swords of imperial troops, saw blood crimson the streets of Alexandria, hid from his foes in boats and tents. Fellow bishops slandered him, charged him with murder and black magic. Five times he was exiled; and in exile we discover him in Rome and Milan and Gaul, in Antioch and Constan-tinople, in the city and the desert, in half the civilized world—always in peril yet never afraid, ever harassed yet serenely confident that truth will triumph. In the midst of all this he wrote letters and he wrote books—history and theology and apologetics—always with authority, ever the hammer of a hated heresy. And when he died in 373— quietly, in bed—he could know that under God he had destroyed Arianism in the East, had preserved for Chris-tianity the core of its message: Jesus Christ is God.

For the thinking Christian, Athanasius poses a problem. The problem, put simply, is . . . sanctity and activity. How can an Athanasius, immersed in administration, entangled with emperors, "in journeyings often, in perils in the city, in perils in the wilderness, in perils in the sea, in perils from false brethren, in labor and hardships, in many sleepless nights, in hunger and thirst, in cold and nakedness" (2 Cor 11:26-27), how can a man totally committed to this world be absorbed in God? What fellowship can he claim with the martyr Ignatius and the hermit Antony?

I shall grapple with the problem in three stages. The three stages are, in substance, the three points I made when I wrote of sanctity and martyrdom, when I wrote of sanctity and solitude. In the Christian scheme of things, active life in the world is, first, a valid way to God, to personal sanctity; it is, second, a unique witness to Christian truth; it is, third, a source of sanctification for others.

In the first place, active life in the world is a valid way to God, to personal sanctity. Not just *any* activity, of course. After all, activity is merely some manner of motion, of movement: the tongue in motion, the legs in motion, the hands in motion, and so on. But motion, movement, can bring a man close to God or take him far from God. Pontius Pilate was highly active on the first Good Friday; and yet he gave Christ over to be crucified. Athanasius, on the other hand, consecrated his actions to a defense of divinity; he refused to hand Christ over to His enemies. The least we can ask of activity, the first demand we make on it, is that a man's actions be not bad, immoral, unworthy in themselves. They must be capable of leading a man to God. Blasphemy will not; prayer can. Fornication will not; marriage can.

But that is not quite enough. A priest is not holy just because he holds a host aloft each day. A theologian is not holy just because he writes about God. A married man is not holy just because marriage is a holy state, a symbol of the union between Christ and His Church. Holiness makes a second demand on activity: a demand on a man's motive, on the reason why he acts. If I am to be one with God, if I am to grow in oneness, my motives must not remain natural, tied to this world. A child kneeling in chapel, but only because teacher is punishing him; a teen-ager avoiding bad company, but only because he fears his father's anger; a girl skirting passion, but only because she dreads pregnancy;

a politician at a wake, but only because
a wake means a vote; a businessman who
will not defraud his customers, but only
because a man-made code forbids it—
these motives may not be sinful, but they
are insufficient, inadequate. Inadequate
because they leave no room for God. If
my activity—be it an isolated gesture or
my habitual occupation—is to generate
oneness with God, then my motives cannot be divorced from God—God as I
know Him through faith, God as He
has disclosed Himself in the Old Testament and the New. And here the possibilities are broad. I can shun sin from
a saving fear of God's just judgments as
evidenced in hell-fire. I can feed the
hungry and clothe the naked out of
reverence for the image of God that is
man. I can keep all ten commandments
because in the God of Sinai my happiness and my heaven lie. Or I can live
the Christian life out of selfless love:
because God is God, because He is
Goodness personified. The motives are
many; but, on broad lines, the less of
self there is in my motivation, the more
room there is for God; and the more God
dominates my drive towards God, the
closer will be my oneness with Him.

A third element, and the most vital,
is God's grace. All holiness, all oneness
with God, *starts* with God: God takes

the initiative; uncompelled, He gives me a small share in His life. Without it, my activity is pagan. My motive will never rise above the natural, my activity will never transcend this world, unless God enlightens my mind so that I may know His mind, unless God strengthens my will so that I may do His will. And I will not do His will consistently unless God is present within me as the abiding principle of my godlikeness, the permanent force that makes me and my actions holy.

Activity, motive, grace—the uncommon sanctity of Athanasius consists of his having fused these three elements in extraordinary fashion. He was splendidly active: few voices in Christendom have thundered so long and so far, so fearlessly and so successfully, that Christ is genuinely God. His motives were magnificently Christian: unflinching faith in the God-man, sacrificial love for the Lord he defended, deep devotion to the images of Christ whose faith and love the Arian conflict imperiled. And all this was the transfiguring work of grace: God living in him, God active in him, sharpening his mind to cut to the heart of the heresy, fortifying his will to stand undismayed against the world.

So then, a life of activity, under God's

grace, is a valid way to personal holiness. My second point: the active life is a unique witness to Christian truth, to Christ. The point is this. If a life of consecrated solitude recaptures the hidden life of Christ, a life of consecrated activity reproduces the public life of Christ. But what our Lord preached in His public life can be summed up in a single sentence of His: "The kingdom of God is at hand" (Mk 1:15). What Christ came to announce was God's dominion, His rule over men, His absolute sovereignty. God is King; we are His people. This divine dominion, Christ insisted, is universal; it is spiritual; it is visible. It is universal: there are no national limits, no boundaries of blood; all men are summoned to serve the King. It is spiritual: under the direction of the Holy Spirit, men redeemed by Christ will be led to interior righteousness, to oneness with God, to holiness. It is visible: those who accept God's rule form a community apart; they are gathered into a Church, whose function is to incorporate all God's children into one body, to make it possible for them to live a life of faith and hope and love under God, and so prepare for God's final coming, His rule over men at the end of time, into eternity.

This task of preaching the kingdom,

of announcing that God's dominion over men is at hand, that His rule is universal, spiritual, and visible, this task begun by Christ is prolonged by His Church. Some men, a relatively small proportion of the Christian body, are specially ordained for that purpose. Official representative of the Church, an Athanasius proclaims Christ by "the ministry of the word." But every Christian, cleric or lay, has been commissioned by his baptism and confirmation to bear witness to Christ. Member of the Church, he is by his Christian profession a prophet: he is in duty bound to announce God's kingship by the fullness of his Christian life. His love, unlimited this side of hell, will proclaim more vividly than words that all men are God's people—black or white, Russian or American, Jew or gentile, Catholic or Protestant, atheist or agnostic. His whole manner of life— human, yet lived on a level above the human—will proclaim that man's primary concern must be spiritual: he must submit himself so unreservedly to God's sovereignty, to the action of the Spirit, that day by day he moves to closer intimacy with God. His devotion to the Church will proclaim that a living, throbbing, visible organism holds in its care the sacraments and Sacrifice which link men to God.

Yes, Christian activity, under God's grace, is a valid way to personal holiness, and it is a unique witness to Christ. And precisely for that reason my third affirmation is so true: Christian activity is a source of sanctification for others. This is fairly obvious where the activity is priestly: Athanasius flaying the Arian heresy; Chrysostom castigating corruption from his pulpit in Constantinople; Xavier hunting souls 75,000 miles, averaging ten conversions to the mile; the Curé of Ars absolving from sin eighteen hours a day; John Bosco educating boys to Christian perfection; the thousands of parish priests who pillow Christ on trembling tongues day in and day out. It is not so obvious where lay activity is concerned; but, obvious or not, it is undeniable: Christianity, when lived, is a magnet; incarnate in an individual, it may prove irresistible. In fact, I suspect that more souls are drawn to Christ by warm example than by cold logic; more minds are attracted to truth that is lived than to truth that is preached.

I have before me a book entitled *Where I Found Christ*.[1] Fourteen converts tell their intimate story. Each story is a search—a search for ultimate mean-

[1] John A. O'Brien, ed., *Where I Found Christ* (Garden City, N.Y.: Doubleday & Company, Inc., 1950).

33

ing, for God. It is remarkable how often the search is shaped or simplified by example: Catholics who are gay about their religion . . . a lovely coed tiptoeing from a dormitory to Mass on a weekday morning . . . a congregation prayerfully fingering its beads . . . the wheel chairs at Lourdes . . . Hawthorne's daughter founding a refuge for the cancerous poor. And Raïssa Maritain tells how she and her husband Jacques were profoundly moved by the famous French author, Léon Bloy; how they asked of him not controversy, not discussion, "only the example of his life, a trusting, tranquil communication, in terms that were his own, of what he believed, of what he loved, of what he held for the absolute truth." [2]

One final caution. Activity is perilous and profitless in the measure that it is divorced from God. That is why activity, man's gaze fixed on the world, must have for companion contemplation, man's gaze fixed on God. Athanasius knew that. At sixty he spent six years, his third exile, in the desert with Antony the Hermit and with the monks of Egypt; he lived their life. God needs men, yes; such is His design for redemption. "No man enters heaven all by him-

[2] *Ibid.*, p. 210.

self." [3] But God takes no joy in sheer activity. If your life is to lead you to Christ, if it is to bear witness to Christ, if it is to draw others to Christ, there is one demand you dare not disregard: you must love God above all else, you must love all others as Christ our Lord has loved you.

[3] Thomas Merton, in John A. O'Brien, *ibid.,* p. 239.

st. augustine
sanctity and conversion

EVERY conversion is high spiritual drama. For most, the drama is played out at the interior of the soul; it is not the stuff of which headlines are made. But every so often the man and the moment conspire, history hangs breathless in the balance, and God breaks almost visibly into His world.

So it was with a remarkable Roman in fourth-century Africa. No single thinker has influenced Western culture so profoundly and on so many fronts as has Augustine. Standing on the ruins of antiquity, this many-faceted man laid the intellectual and spiritual heritage of the old world at the feet of the new in a vast synthesis. And yet, till he was thirty-two, Augustine was just another bright young man in tortured quest of truth and love, his heart restless because it did not rest in God. Born to a Christian mother and a pagan father, unbaptized, with only a superficial knowledge of Christ and Christianity, Augustine confronted two major crises quite unprepared. One crisis was moral, the other intellectual.

The moral crisis began when Augustine was fifteen: "Arrived now at adolescence I burned for all the satisfactions of hell, and I sank to the animal in a succession of dark lusts." [1] At sixteen he came to semipagan Carthage; there "a cauldron of illicit loves leapt and boiled about me. I was not yet in love, but I was in love with love. . . ." [2] At seventeen he took a mistress, lived with her for thirteen years, had a son by her, surrendered her with sorrow: "My heart . . . was broken and wounded and shed blood." [3] During this prolonged crisis Augustine's prayer to God was: " 'Grant me chastity and continence, but not yet.' For I was afraid that you would hear my prayer too soon, and too soon would heal me. . . ." [4]

The intellectual crisis began when Augustine was eighteen. He had read Cicero, and from that moment he thirsted for truth and wisdom. This

[1] St. Augustine, *Confessions* 2, 1; trans. F. J. Sheed, *The Confessions of St. Augustine* (New York: Sheed & Ward, 1943), p. 27.
[2] *Confessions* 3, 1; tr. Sheed, p. 41.
[3] *Confessions* 6, 15; tr. Sheed, p. 126.
[4] *Confessions* 8, 7; tr. Sheed, p. 170.

38

truth and wisdom he sought in Scripture; but the Bible repelled him: it was too simple, could not compare with the majesty of Cicero. Catholicism seemed naive—good enough for his mother Monica, unworthy of an intellectual. What beguiled him was Manicheism, the religion of the Persian prophet Mani. Manichean propaganda proved a powerful magnet. It lured his intellectualism, for it claimed to be scientific, a revelation demonstrated by reason, a free philosophy without the bridle of faith. It tempted the sophisticate: here was salvation through secret knowledge. It preserved the relics of his childhood religion: here was a superior, perfect form of Christianity, completing the revelation of Christ. It touched an inner torment: perhaps the origin of evil could be explained by two Principles at war, the Good and the Evil. It appealed to his pride, for it absolved him from moral guilt: a strange Principle, another nature, was reponsible for his sin. "It pleased my pride to be free from blame." [5]

It took ten years of Manicheism to disenchant Augustine. Even then orthodox Christianity did not seem the answer. Skepticism tempted him lightly. And he still had to learn that a captivat-

[5] *Confessions* 5, 10; translation mine.

ing philosophy, Neoplatonism, did not possess the two truths he needed, the twin truths he found in St. Paul: a God who saves man by becoming man, and a grace which alone gives victory over sin. And even when he had discovered the Saviour Christ and His grace, it was Augustine's intellect that was captured; his will was not completely conquered —the pull of the flesh was still too powerful.

The drama reached its climax in August of 386. The city was Milan, the scene a little garden. "There I was, going mad on my way to sanity, dying on my way to life, aware how evil I was, unaware that I was to grow better in a little while." [6] Pleasure plucked at his garment of flesh, murmuring softly: "Are you sending us away?" Chastity smiled on him and gave him courage: "Cast yourself upon the Lord and be not afraid." Conscious of his sinfulness, he was torn by violent tears and flung himself down beneath a fig tree: "How long shall I go on saying 'tomorrow'?"

". . . And suddenly I heard a voice from some nearby house, a boy's voice or a girl's voice, I do not know; but it was a sort of sing-song, repeated again and again, 'Take and read, take and

[6] *Confessions* 8, 8; tr. Sheed, p. 171.

read.' . . . Damming back the flood of my tears I arose, interpreting the incident as quite certainly a divine command to open my book of Scripture and read the passage at which I should open. . . . I snatched it up, opened it and in silence read the passage upon which my eyes first fell: 'not in revelry and drunkenness, not in debauchery and wantonness, not in strife and jealousy; but put on the Lord Jesus Christ, and as for the flesh, take no thought for its lusts' (Rom 13:13-14). I had no wish to read further, and no need. For in that instant, with the very ending of the sentence, it was as though a light of utter confidence shone in all my heart, and all the darkness of uncertainty vanished away." [7]

Almost nine months later, on the night between Holy Saturday and Easter Sunday, 387, Augustine was baptized by the Bishop of Milan, St. Ambrose. That night the oil of confirmation completed his baptism, and for the first time Augustine pillowed on his tongue the Christ he had fled "down the arches of the years."

The conversion of Augustine is uncommonly suggestive for an understand-

[7] *Confessions* 8, 12; tr. Sheed, pp. 178-79; version of Romans 13:13-14 taken from Confraternity edition.

41

ing of sanctity. All conversion is change, a turning. Conversion to Christianity is a turning to Christ. In the Catholic view of things, this turning to Christ takes place within the Body of Christ, within the Church. Sanctity, I shall suggest, involves a triple turning; oneness with God comprises a threefold conversion to Christ.

Sanctity involves, first, a basic, radical conversion. The more obvious case of radical conversion is the person we call a "convert." An adult, an Augustine, for the first time surrenders his mind completely to Christ: "I believe in one God the Father; and in one Lord Jesus Christ, His only Son; and in the Holy Spirit. I believe in one, holy, catholic, apostolic Church." An adult for the first time turns his will totally to Christ and in infinite sadness exclaims with Augustine: "*Late* have I loved thee, O Beauty so ancient, O Beauty so new; *late* have I loved thee!" [8] Water bathes his brow, and he is caught up into a new life. A life that is faith: seeing life through the eyes of Christ. A life that is hope: living life on firm trust in the grace of Christ. A life that is love: loving the Life that is Christ within him. This is basic Christian holiness: oneness with God through the indwelling of Christ.

[8] *Confessions* 10, 27; translation mine.

42

Less obvious, but still basic, is another conversion. I mean, the "born Catholic," the "born Christian." In point of fact, there is no such creature. A child is not born Christian; he is made Christian. Earth's loveliest infant lacks something basic at birth: he lacks Christ; our Lord has not yet made His home within him. That is the task of his christening.

Regrettably, we have lost the original meaning of the word "christen." Christen once meant to Christianize, to make a Christian. A child's christening does precisely that: it makes a child Christian, Christlike. For it roots Christ in him, and it roots in him remarkable powers: power to say "I believe you" in response to God's revelation, power to say "I hope in you" in reply to God's promises, power to say "I love you" in answer to God's self-giving. Oh yes, only the years will bring these powers to life. There is the touching moment when a child makes his first deliberate act of faith, his first conscious act of hope, his first human act of love. There is the crisis when a young man must choose between the Christ of his cradle days and the rival gods that beckon so imperiously, so seductively. But these only confirm a conversion which long since turned him to Christ. Infant baptism is a con-

43

version, because it changes a child of
earth into a child of God, a mere infant
into a holy innocent. This is basic Christian holiness: oneness with God through
the indwelling of Christ.

The first phase of Christian sanctity,
therefore, is a radical conversion:
through baptism Christ makes His home
in a soul, and an infant or an adult becomes a living member of Christ's Body.
This root conversion takes place once.
But a second phase, another conversion,
follows upon the first, and it is a more
frequent thing. For even when baptism
has destroyed Adam's sin in us, a legacy
from that sin abides in us—what the
Church so vividly calls the "touchwood,"
the "tinder," of sin. It is the native attraction which evil has for fallen nature,
even after Christ has possessed that nature. Before I can say yes or no, my flesh
is inflamed by forbidden fruit, my mind
is invaded by pride or envy, by doubt
or rebellion, by thoughts that scandalize
me.

Augustine was aware of that. Ten
years after his baptism he had to confess
that he was still wrestling with the lust
of the flesh, the lust of the eyes, and the
pride of life: with the memory of illicit
love, the allurement of beauty sundered
from Loveliness supreme, "the desire to
be feared and loved by men for no other

44

reason than the joy I get from it." [9]

In all this temptation, in all such seduction, there is no sin unless I freely say yes. But if I do say yes, I have willingly turned my heart to a creature. And if I turn so completely to a creature that I turn away from Christ, another conversion is imperative—each time I turn away—else sanctity is impossible, for union has been destroyed. I must turn away from the creature, I must turn again to Christ. Here the conversion is not baptism but confession; here sanctity comes not through water but through sorrow.

So much for the radical conversion that is baptism; so much for the essential conversion that is repentance. There is a third conversion, which has little to do with sin and much with sanctity, a conversion to Christ which never ceases. What is given in baptism, what is restored in repentance, is life—a share in God's life. Therefore you must grow; for if you cease to grow, eventually you begin to die. Without losing your identity, you must turn more and more Christlike, more and more godlike, every day.

Here again Augustine is instructive. His baptism was but a beginning. In a

[9] *Confessions* 10, 36; tr. Sheed, p. 249.

monastic setting of his own making, he
fixed his gaze on God for more than
two years. This solitude he surrendered
to serve God's people. His burdens as
bishop were crushing: liturgy and administration, sermons and correspond-
ence, charity and orthodoxy, baptismal
instruction and spiritual direction,
Church councils and episcopal courts
—at a time when he was writing book
after masterful book. And still he organized in the shadow of his cathedral
a sort of monastery where he shared with
clerics a life of poverty, chastity, and
asceticism. His secret he has revealed:
"Love your neighbor; then look inside
yourself at what you love him with; and
there you will see . . . God." [10]

The point is: your conversion to Christ
will be always more complete, the more
Christlike you make your every moment.
This demands, first, contemplation.
Every so often you must be alone with
God; for if you are to have increasingly
the mind of Christ, you must grow consistently in knowledge of Him. Second,
your activity, like all authentically
Christian activity, must be rooted in
God's grace and in a motive not of this
earth. It will be most Christian if a
child of God, with the grace of God,

[10] St. Augustine, *On the Gospel of John* 17, 8.

does all for love of God. Third, you dare not be content with a minimum; you dare not say venial sin is unimportant. If perfection is your purpose, every imperfection is reason for Christian regret.

Christianity is not a Sunday-morning nod to God; it is Calvary thrilling through each moment. Sanctity is not folded hands and bent head; it is the risen Christ living in you now. Morality is not just chastity and an Index of Forbidden Books; it is a loving faith that cannot be contained, that does not ask, what must I do to stay out of sin? but rather, what more can I do for Him who has done so much for me?

It is this sort of conversion—begun at baptism, repaired by repentance, perfected through the bittersweet of earthly living—that touches the Catholic ideal of high holiness. Its consummation will be an eternal conversion, when the risen Christian faces the risen Christ in endless contemplation, in ceaseless love.

st. jerome

sanctity and passion

THE STORY persists that a Renaissance Pope once came upon a painting of St. Jerome. It was one of those portraits that picture Jerome in the desert, gaunt and wild-eyed, on his knees before a human skull, beating his breast with a stone. And the Pope, we are told, exclaimed: "Ah, Jerome! Had you not been discovered in that posture, you would not be on the Church's altars today!" The story points up a problem—a problem that is incarnate in St. Jerome, and that has important implications for Christian sanctity.

Jerome is something of a paradox. On the one hand, he is admirable. We find in Jerome a humanist whom the Renaissance revered, one so steeped in classical culture that he confessed he could no more forget it than the wine jar can lose the flavor of the wine,

one so enamored of Latin literature
that he dreamt himself haled before
Christ on the charge: "You are not a
Christian, you are a Ciceronian." [1] We
find a Scripture scholar, expert in
Hebrew, expert in Greek, a master of
translation, with a love for God's word
that is summarized in his own advice:
When your head droops at night, let a
page of Scripture pillow it.[2] We find
an ascetic who lived his last thirty-four
years in Bethlehem, in the shadow of a
manger, linking scholarship with monastic life: "Having food and raiment
I shall be satisfied, and the naked cross
I shall naked follow." [3] We find an exciting controversialist, sometimes wrong
but never dull, breaking lances with
heretics and orthodox, on marriage and
virginity, on solitude and celibacy, on
grace and the Trinity, on the meaning
of Scripture. We find in Jerome the most
learned man of the fourth century, perhaps the most erudite figure in Christian
antiquity.

On the other hand, Jerome is deeply
puzzling. For we find in Jerome a man
of strong feelings, a sensitive, passionate
human being. The heart of the matter
is his frank self-analysis: "I have no

[1] St. Jerome, *Letter* 22, 30.
[2] Cf. *Letter* 22, 17.
[3] *Letter* 52, 5.

breast of iron, no heart of stone. I was not born of flint, was not suckled by Hyrcanian tigers." [4]

In the first place, Jerome was quick to be hurt. He was petulant when Augustine questioned the value of his Old Testament translation from the Hebrew. He was distressed when monks of the desert called him heretic for his conception of the Trinity. He was wounded when his relations with a noble Roman ascetic, Paula, were misinterpreted. He was violent when a priest, Vigilantius, taxed him with his devotion to a controverted Christian writer named Origen. He brooded when his friends failed to write; he censured them when their letters were short.

Second, Jerome was slow to forgive. He left the desert bitter; his attitude: "it is better to dwell amid wild beasts than with such Christians." [5] He left Rome embittered; in his books Christian Rome was "Babylon." [6] The death of a former friend, Rufinus, prompted a raw valedictory: "Now that the scorpion lies buried in [Sicily] . . . and the hydra with its numerous heads has ceased its hissing against us . . . I will tackle the prophet Ezekiel." [7]

[4] *Letter 14*, 3.
[5] *Letter 17*, 3.
[6] *Letter 45*, 6.
[7] Preface to *Commentary on Ezekiel*.

Third, Jerome's attacks on sin, on error, on hypocrisy, were dipped in mordant satire. He antagonized clerics by reminding them of a Greek proverb: "A fat paunch never breeds fine thoughts." [8] He assailed fasting women who "cover up their faces but manage to leave one eye open to watch the effect." [9] He warned consecrated virgins not to seek their Bridegroom "in the city squares." [10] He could question a man's motives as well as his orthodoxy, jest at his origins as well as his ignorance: he called Vigilantius an innkeeper who cut his wine with water in his tavern and in his theology.

Fourth, his very asceticism brought out Jerome's very human reactions. Two years he spent in the desert, blackened by a blazing sun. Lonely, he begged for letters. A gourmet with a weak stomach, he found desert food a penance. Even when his companions were scorpions and wild animals, his mind was invaded by "bands of dancing girls." [11]

Jerome's most sympathetic biographers find him an "irascible hermit." They know he fought his feelings, but they admit that often he failed. They

[8] *Letter 52*, 11.
[9] *Letter 22*, 27.
[10] *Letter 22*, 25.
[11] *Letter 22*, 7.

52

know that only death arrested his ceaseless search for perfection, but they admit that only death stilled the surging cry of his passions.

Such is, in sum, the story of Jerome. The story points up a fact which gives rise to a problem. The fact is . . . passion. In man there are two sets of appetites: rational appetites and sense appetites. I have emotions, and I have strong feelings or passions.

I have rational appetites, emotions. I mean the response of my soul, the reaction of my will, to what is set before it. I watch Tchaikovsky's *Swan Lake Ballet*, and my soul delights in it; or I listen to Fauré's *Requiem*, and my soul is sad. I am ill, and my spirit yearns for health; or I picture hell-fire, and my spirit shrinks from it. I contemplate Christ, and I am suffused with love; I recall Judas, and I detest his treachery. But I am not pure spirit; I have sense appetites, strong feelings, passions. I mean the response of my body, the reaction of my flesh, to an object that comes to my knowledge—say to something I see or hear or touch or taste or smell. A stranger insults me, and my face flushes with rage. I smell smoke, and I pale with fear. I spy a lovely woman, and my heartbeats quicken with desire. I eat Lobster Cardinal, and my taste buds thrill. I am slapped, and my muscles tense with hate.

And because man is a unified creature, not flesh strapped to spirit, it is often the whole man—not just the soul or just the body—that responds to what he knows. The fear in my soul makes my limbs tremble; my soul's sorrow finds an outlet in tears; impure desires inflame my flesh; rich pleasure in a symphony or a sunset is my total being aglow!

That is the fact, and out of the fact springs a problem. What role have the feelings in human living? What part does passion play in a Christ-redeemed world, in sanctity?

On broad lines, there are two extreme positions and a Christian middle. One extreme is an Anglo-Saxon legacy: passion is something to be ashamed of. For strong feeling is a sign of weakness; the manly reaction to reality is stoicism. Love, of course, but let not love enrapture you, let it not glow. Be afraid, if you must, but keep your teeth from chattering. Take joy from a sonata, but let it not thrill you. Death will always sadden, but you dare not weep. Detest sin, but never be disturbed by it. Protest injustice, but grow not black with anger.

The opposite extreme insists that passion is man at his best. To be completely

human is to let the flesh have its way
—not to give the spirit exclusive sway.
After all, man is more animal than angel.
Let him, therefore, thrill to all that is
delightful, lust to satiety. Let fear spend
him, and hate exhaust him. Let him
weep and rage to his heart's content.
It is fear of the flesh that emasculates;
it is frustration of the flesh that sprouts
the ills of the spirit.

Midway between these two extremes
stands the Christian position. Passion is
natural, yes. Where you find a man, you
can expect to find feelings. For man is
not simply spirit; he has a body. And
because the body is alive, it has its appetites; it responds to what is pleasurable or painful; it has its attachments
and its aversions. Physically, passion is
a good thing: it is part of my equipment
as man, it is God-given, it is intended
by God to help me achieve my destiny.
Why, even the God-man had strong
feelings. He wept—over Jerusalem and
over Lazarus, over His city and His
friend. He drove money-changers from
the Temple with a whip, because ardor
for His Father's house consumed Him;
and it may well be that, as Jerome suggests, "fire gleamed in His eyes." And
in His agony "His sweat became as
drops of blood running down upon the
ground" (Lk 22:44).

And yet, if passion is to rise above the animal, if it is to be not only physically but morally good, it must be made human. But passion is human only to the extent that it is subject to reason, modulated by will. Here man will never be a dictator. I cannot say to my flesh: "I forbid you to take pleasure in what is pleasurable, to be pained by what is painful. Henceforth beauty will never ravish you, depravity never disgust you. You will not be warmed by desire or chilled by fear. Ridiculed, you will not bristle; tempted, you will not tingle. Hope will cease to electrify you, sorrow to leaden your step."

No, I am not a dictator; I cannot destroy my feelings. But I can be their master; I can exercise a significant control. If I cannot say, "Passion, never arise!", I can say, "Thus far, and no further!" I cannot bar passion from entering my flesh; I can keep it from overpowering my spirit.

The solution is a task of reason, a work of will, and a gift of grace. It is the task of reason to discover what objects of passion are legitimate for me, in my circumstances—what feelings I may encourage, what feelings I must discourage. To rage against God because cancer has ravaged my child may be spontaneous, but it is never justifiable

—for anyone. The passionate yearning of a husband for his wife is splendidly Christian; but the case is far different for a monk vowed to chastity. Sorrow can be a good thing, if it is measured by the object of my grief and does not destroy me. After all, St. Peter wept bitterly upon denying his Lord; and Augustine's sentence is a minor classic: If anyone "sees it as sin that for so small a portion of an hour I wept for my mother, now dead and departed from my sight, who had wept so many years for me that I should live ever in your sight—let him not scorn me but rather, if he is a man of great charity, let him weep for my sins to you. . . ." [12]

But if it is the task of my reason to discern the licit lengths of passion, it is the work of my will to control it. This is where passion meets morality—in the deliberate decisions of my will. Here is where desire and desperation become more than facts of the flesh; here is where courage and hate become good or bad in God's sight. I feel a surge of anger; I am titillated by desire; I am sodden with despair—this is the animal in me. Now I recognize that this rage is out of all proportion, this desire is not for me, despair is death—this is the

[12] St. Augustine, *Confessions* 9, 12; tr. Sheed, *op. cit.*, p. 205.

rational in me. And so I vow that I will reduce my wrath to proper balance, I will turn my thoughts from the sensual, I will hope as long as I have life—this is the moral in me.

All this is highly human, but it is not yet Christian. To be Christian, controlled passion must lead me to Christ. To lead me to Christ, it needs the grace of Christ. Concretely, I need, first, God's light for my mind, so that I may grasp without confusion the legitimate limits of passion. I need, second, God's strength for my will, so that I may imprison passion within those limits. I need, above all, God Himself within me, so that I may harness passion to my quest for perfection, so that, paradoxically, passion may increase my intimacy, my oneness, with God.

There is a tendency among devout people to see in passion nothing save an obstacle to sanctity. The attitude is not Christian. I do not deny that passion is a perilous possession; but it is no more dangerous than reason or free will. Adam proved that. The point is: all the drive behind human activity stems from the emotions of my soul and the feelings of my flesh. Unleashed, they destroy; mastered, they sanctify.

In a word, the stronger the passions and emotions, the greater the possibilities for good or evil, for sanctity or damnation. A remarkable example is Jerome. Some of his feelings we dare not condone; he was not faultless. Some of his reactions we shall not understand this side of eternity; he is too complex. But Christian tradition has canonized his life as a whole, assures us that he harnessed passion to reason in striking fashion. A less unruly nature might have spelled more peace; I doubt that it would have realized such resounding achievements for God and for humanity.

One final thought. The perfection of sanctity on earth will come when spirit and flesh respond in harmony to the indwelling of God. This truth has been captured in sparkling verse by a perceptive nun:

> It's this that makes
>   My spirit spin,
> My bones to quake,
>   My blood run thin,
> My flesh to melt
>   Inside my skin,
> My very pulse
>   Create a din—
> It's this that makes
>   My spirit spin:
>
> That Heaven is
>   Not *up*, but *in!* [13]

[13] Sister Mary Ignatius, "Discovery," *Messenger of the Sacred Heart*, 77, No. 2 (Feb., 1942) 58.

st. martín de porres

sanctity and color

 N LIMA, Peru, on December 9, 1579, a mulatto was born. Illegitimate son of a Spanish grandee, John de Porres, and a free Negress, Anna Velásquez, his skin was black—so black that for some years his father would not acknowledge him, and the baptismal register in the Church of St. Sebastian read: "Martin, son of an unknown father." At twelve he apprenticed himself to a *barbero* or *cirujano*—in those days a combination of barber, pharmacist, doctor, and surgeon—and began a medical apostolate among the poor. At fifteen or sixteen he was accepted by the Friars Preachers, the Dominicans, as a lay helper. He swept cells and cloisters and corridors, cleaned toilets, cut hair, and was something of a physician and surgeon. He prayed long hours, slept rarely, fasted much. Nine years later, his

61

superiors and the entire Dominican community, intensely moved by Martin's penance and prayer, his lowliness and his love, persuaded him to make full profession as a religious.

Martin's thirty-five years as a Dominican brother were quite extraordinary. Extraordinary not so much because he had visions and ecstasies, never ate meat, lashed himself three times a night with a whip whose hooked ends were weighted with iron. Extraordinary rather because this half-Spanish, half-Negro Peruvian loved all men with an astonishing love, served his city and his monastery with utter unconcern for race, color, or station. He distributed more than two thousand dollars a week in food and clothing to Lima's poor, filled the beds of the Dominican infirmary with the sick and dying he found lying in the streets, founded an orphanage and foundling hospital. And in an hour of financial crisis he asked his superior to sell him into slavery if it would provide for the needs of the brothers he loved. All this because he saw in every human being not a color but Christ, not festering sores but the wounds of his Lord; because he realized that every human frame is another Calvary, where a human person is playing out the passion of Christ, making up in his own flesh what is still wanting to the sufferings of his Saviour.[1]

On May 6, 1962, Martin de Porres was canonized, was officially declared a saint of the Catholic Church. It was his life, of course, and not his color that brought him such uncommon honor; but just as clearly his canonization is remarkably relevant: it gives us what someone has called "the saint for our own time." For in the second half of the twentieth century, in a country relatively religious and surprisingly sophisticated, increasingly liberal and presumably purged of age-old myths, we still have to persuade not only atheists but Christians as well, first, that the Negro is a human being; second, that the Negro has been redeemed by Christ; and third, that the Negro is capable of high holiness, of sanctity.

The Negro is a human being. I mean, he has been fashioned by God with a mind to know and a heart to love. He is a person. He can transfer to himself what Shakespeare's Shylock said of the Jews: "Has not a Negro eyes? Has not a Negro hands, organs, dimensions, senses, affections, passions? Fed with the same food, hurt with the same weap-

[1] For the details of Martin's life, see Giuliana Cavallini, *St. Martin de Porres, Apostle of Charity,* trans. Caroline Holland (St. Louis: Herder, 1963).

ons, subject to the same diseases, healed by the same means, warmed and cooled by the same winter and summer as a white man is? If you prick us, do we not bleed? If you tickle us, do we not laugh? If you poison us, do we not die? If you wrong us, shall we not revenge? If we are like you in the rest, we will resemble you in that." [2]

As a human being, the Negro shares the contemporary awareness, the new realization of sensitive men everywhere, that to be human a man must be free: free to breathe without constriction, to dream his dreams with some hope for their actualization, to speak his thoughts and sing his songs without fear of reprisal, to walk the same sidewalks with the white man and share the same pew, to learn what his fellow man learns, to work not only in toilets but at tasks that ennoble the human spirit, to watch his children grow not in stultifying slums but in civilized decency.

Moreover, with his history and his wounds and his memories, the Negro is perhaps more passionately athirst for freedom than any other race. For he knows what it means *not* to be free, what it means to be a slave. He knows what it does to the human spirit to sit

[2] Cf. *The Merchant of Venice*, Act 3, Scene 1.

always in the back of a bus, to be pushed into the gutter, to live in filth, to be barred from hotels and restaurants, from movie houses and rest rooms, from so much of human living, because he is black. Not because he is ignorant, not because he is dirty, not because he is penniless—only because he is black.

The problem is fearfully complex, with some of its elements hidden in history. For one thing, as a practicing psychiatrist has put it, "The essence of the problem we face is not race and not color. American people, by a coercive slavery system and by miscegenation, grossly altered American Negroes into a group whose characteristics were so shaped as to prevent their participation in the American life as defined by the Bill of Rights and the Constitution. What used to be a slave group containing stock from several races has been perpetuated as a low caste servant and labor group, for the most part isolated in its compound. The color primarily helps us to identify the low caste and to know whom we should not touch. When a Caucasian and a Negro can together produce a child who is called a Negro, we are dealing with sociological rather than logical thinking. Such thinking is one of the many residuals of slave culture days. It ensures that the low caste elements remain clearly defined no matter how intermixed and unrecognizable they become. It also contains the implicit censure that whosoever touches one becomes one. To be born in the compound is to feel inferior, to behave as if one is inferior and, in some instances, to be trained to be inferior." [3]

The problem of the Negro in American life is complex, but despite all its complexity there is one truth we dare not deny: the Negro is a person, a human being, fashioned by God to His own image, destined to live in oneness and equality with his fellow man. Do not tell me that the Old Testament refutes all this, that God cursed the Negro, segregated black from white, made him inferior to the rest of mankind, congenitally and insuperably and endlessly low on the pole of humanity. This is scriptural nonsense, and they who propagate it are not preaching the Word of God.

Yes, it is the task of every man to realize that a Negro is human, as human as any man, possessed of the same yearn-

[3] Charles Pinderhughes, M.D., "Psychological Effects of Segregation," *Catholic Mind*, 63, No. 1192 (April, 1965), 7-8. The article (pp. 4-8) is taken from a *Report on Racial Imbalance in the Boston Public Schools* by the Massachusetts State Advisory Committee to the United States Commission on Civil Rights, January, 1965.

66

ing and the same right to be free. But
the Christian must go one step further:
he must grasp the simple but profound
truth that the Negro has been redeemed
by Christ, that the Negro's vocation is to
the freedom whereby Christ has made us
free. St. Paul's affirmation to the Galatians, "There is neither Jew nor Greek,
neither slave nor freeman, neither male
nor female, for you are all one in Christ
Jesus" (Gal 3:28), can be legitimately
extended and brought up to date:
"There is neither white nor Negro."
This is not to deny the reality of race,
of color; but it does affirm that, in the
eyes of God, race and color are without Christian significance. True, Paul
is speaking of the baptized, of Christians: "all you who have been baptized
into Christ, have put on Christ" (Gal
3:27); but it is still true that, with the
very coming of Christ, with His death
and resurrection, *all* men became, in
some initial sense, His brothers.

The Fathers of the Church, the early
Christian writers, were uncommonly
aware of this. They insisted that, at the
moment of Mary's whispered yes, the
unique moment when divinity and humanity were wed in the womb of a
virgin, a basic, radical, fundamental
kinship with God was realized by all
humanity. The thesis was trumpeted

in the West by St. Hilary of Poitiers:
"Every man was in Christ Jesus." [4] "He
has taken the body of each of us." [5]
In the East St. Cyril of Alexandria was
remarkably eloquent on the same theme:
"Christ has us in Himself, inasmuch as
He bore our nature, and the Word's
body was called our body." [6] The basic
affirmation is this: a new oneness, a root
unity, between man and God was con-
ceived in Nazareth and brought to birth
in Bethlehem. For thinkers with the
Christian insight of St. Athanasius, "the
world is so truly one whole that when
the Word enters into it and becomes
one of our race, all things take on a
new dignity." [7] Here the point of contact, the meeting ground between God
and man, is the flesh of Christ, His
humanity. In Nazareth and Bethlehem
humanity was not yet the Body of
Christ, alive with His life, thrilling to
His divine touch. But humanity was
ready, was poised on the edge of divinity. No longer was flesh simply the
tinderbox of sin. If it had not yet begun

[4] St. Hilary of Poitiers, *Commentary on Matthew*
2, 5 (*PL* 9, 927).

[5] *Ibid.* 19, 5 (*PL* 9, 1025).

[6] St. Cyril of Alexandria, *Commentary on John*
9, 1 (Pusey 2, 486).

[7] E. Mersch, *The Whole Christ: The Historical
Development of the Doctrine of the Mystical Body
in Scripture and Tradition,* trans. J. R. Kelly
(London: Dennis Dobson, Ltd., 1949), p. 273.

to live with the life of Christ, it all but quivered with His breath. For the flesh that God took is our flesh; in some genuine sense, it is my flesh, your flesh, the Negro's flesh, the flesh of every human being born into this world.

But this radical oneness between God and man effected at the Incarnation in the flesh of Christ was, like the Incarnation itself, only a beginning, a foundation, a pledge of the reality to come. That reality came on Calvary, when the seed planted in Nazareth came to flower; when the Church came forth, like a New Eve, from the side of the New Adam; when the Mystical Body was born from the torn flesh of the Crucified. It was perfected in the resurrection and ascension of Christ, when not an isolated man but human nature rose radiant from the dead and stood splendent before the Father; when not merely the body born of Mary in a manger triumphed over death, but the Body born of Christ on the wood. This Man who stood then and stands now before the Father is colorless; more accurately, he is every shade of color; he is every man.

Oh yes, redemption has to be brought to the individual Negro—but no more than to the individual white. The tragedy and the scandal are that we have so often, so consistently, so ruthlessly kept redemption from touching the Negro: each Christian who quotes the Bible to range God on the side of segregation; each Christian who forces a Negro to the back of a bus or the rear of a church; each Christian who curses a black man as he would a dog; each Christian who keeps the Negro "in his place," in his ghetto, in his hovel; each Christian who says with his tongue or in his heart "Thus far and no farther." And this to a race that seems to have almost a native yearning for God, a race to whom (as an Anglican bishop once observed) adoration comes as naturally as breathing, a race that sings to God songs of heartrending sorrow and limitless love, a race whose Amens and Alleluias so often shatter our comfortable, reluctant religion with their fervor and their passion.

The Negro has been redeemed by the same blood that was poured out for us. The same Christ, the same Good Shepherd, seeks him out, calls to him. But since the risen Christ calls not always in His own person but frequently through us, we Catholics must bear in large measure the guilt of the Negro's estrangement from Christ, or at least from the Christianity that we claim is Christ living on in time and space. If it

71

is my task to play the *man* to the Negro, to be human in his regard, it is even more imperative to play *Christ* to him, to be genuinely Christian in my relations with him. For, on the solemn word of the God-man, *whatever* we do to the least of these His brothers and sisters, we do to Him. There is no escaping the burden of Christian fellowship, save by ceasing to be Christian. And all too many of us have.

Of such uncircumscribed love St. Augustine has spoken powerfully. Our love, he insists, should be utterly catholic, should be offered, as the grace of God is offered, to all: "Love all men, even your enemies. Love them, not because they are your brothers, but that they may become your brothers—so that you may ever burn with brotherly love, whether for him who is already your brother, or for your enemy, that he may by [your] loving become your brother. . . . Even he who does not yet believe in Christ . . . love him, and love him with brotherly love. He is not yet your brother, but you love him precisely that he may be your brother. All our love, therefore, is brotherly love towards Christians, towards all Christ's members." [8]

In sum, then, it is the urgent task of

[8] St. Augustine, *To the Parthians, on the Epistle of John* 10, 7 (*PL* 35, 2059).

72

every human being to realize not only
that the Negro is human, a person, but
that he has been redeemed by Christ,
that the Son of God offered His flesh
on Calvary as much for the Negro as
for the white. A third and final thought:
this human person redeemed by Christ
is capable of high holiness, of union
with God in day-to-day monotony and
in sudden heroism. Martin de Porres
is striking evidence of this. His secret of
sanctity is simple enough: he loved God
above all things, and he looked on each
human being as a brother or sister in
Christ. To him, color was a fact—no more
than that, and no less.

At this critical moment in American
history there is many a Martin de Porres.
There is many a Negro who loves God
with his whole heart and his whole soul
and his whole mind and with all his
strength. And there are even more
Negroes who are potentially holy because they are so passionately in love
with their fellow men, so passionately
that they are willing to die for them.
There are millions of Negroes in this
country who will march—not always
unafraid, but always with courage—into
the jaws of death because only thus will
freedom and equality come to their
brothers and sisters. And as he marches
today, the Negro sings with confidence:
"We shall overcome." With rare excep-

tions, he means that the Negro will change his oppressor, not crush him; he will overcome hate by love, will make brothers out of enemies. All this is not necessarily Christian, but often it is; and even where it is not, Christ is so close to this people in their Gethsemane that His grace is almost palpable. This need not be high-level sanctity, for heroic holiness must focus on God, not simply on the image of God that is man; but selfless love of man is a splendid springboard to sanctity, and from the crucified love of the Negro people saints like Martin are destined to flower more and more.

Saint for our time—Martin is that. But not because his mind was transported in ecstasy; not because his hands had singular power to heal; not primarily because, half Negro and half Caucasian, he bridges two worlds. Rather because, in these hate-filled days, he reveals the transforming power of love. It will not be enough for the Negro to force from his fellow men the freedom that is his due. With this must be linked his Christian burden: to bring love— his love and God's love—to hearts that are bursting with bitterness; to help make black and white not only humanly equal but divinely one—all one in Christ Jesus.

74

st. patrick
sanctity and ancestry

T WAS about the year 410. The place: an unknown town of Roman Britain. A young man in his middle twenties lay fast asleep in the home of his parents. In the course of that night he had a dream—a dream which was to transform history. I should like you to hear it from his own lips:

"And there I saw in the night the vision of a man, whose name was Victoricus, coming as it were from Ireland, with countless letters. And he gave me one of them, and I read the opening words of the letter, which were, 'The voice of the Irish'; and as I read the beginning of the letter I thought that at the same moment I heard their voice . . . and thus did they cry out as with one mouth: 'We ask thee, boy, come and walk among us once more.' And I was quite broken in heart, and could read no further,

75

and so I woke up. Thanks be to God, after many years the Lord gave to them according to their cry." [1]

Such was the celebrated vision of Patrick. I want to tell you three things about that vision. First, what the vision did for the man who had it: Patrick. Second, what the vision did for the country that called him through it: Ireland. Third, what the vision can do for those who recall it today: you and me.

First, what did the vision do for the man who had it, for Patrick? In a word, it changed the entire direction of his life; it transformed him. Actually, there were two stages in that transformation. For his first sixteen years the Patrick who roamed the fields of southwest Britain lived a carefree, careless life. He was a Christian, yes; but so little did his Christianity mean to him that he could later confess: "I did not know the true God." [2] The priests of Britain preached Christ and Christlike living to him, yes; but he lent them his ears and not his heart. He went to school, yes; but it was games that gripped him, not grammar. And once he sinned seri-

[1] St. Patrick, *Confession* 23, trans. Ludwig Bieler, in *Ancient Christian Writers* 17 (Westminster, Md.: Newman Press, 1953), 28.
[2] *Confession* 1; tr. Bieler, p. 21.

ously against his God, "because I was not yet strong." [3]

But one day, when Patrick was sixteen, Irish raiders swooped down on southwest Britain. "I was taken into captivity to Ireland with many thousands of people—and deservedly so, because we turned away from God, and did not keep His commandments, and did not obey our priests, who used to remind us of our salvation." [4] Six years of slavery—but the slavery was a grace, God's hand outstretched in love. The paragraph in which Patrick sums up those six years is touching:

". . . after I came to Ireland—every day I had to tend sheep, and many times a day I prayed—the love of God and His fear came to me more and more, and my faith was strengthened. And my spirit was moved so that in a single day I would say as many as a hundred prayers, and almost as many in the night, and this even when I was staying in the woods and on the mountain; and I used to get up for prayer before daylight, through snow, through frost, through rain, and I felt no harm, and there was no sloth in me . . . because the spirit within me was then fervent." [5]

[3] *Confession* 27; tr. Bieler, p. 29.
[4] *Confession* 1; tr. Bieler, p. 21.
[5] *Confession* 16; tr. Bieler, p. 25.

That was the first stage in the transformation of Patrick: slavery in Ireland. The second stage had to wait his escape from slavery: the vision in Britain, the voice of the Irish pleading with Patrick: "We ask thee, boy, come and walk among us once more." It is a vision that brings to mind inevitably another remarkable vision, the vision of St. Paul in Troas. As St. Luke describes it in the Acts of the Apostles: "Paul had a vision one night. A Macedonian was standing, appealing to him and saying: 'Come over into Macedonia and help us.' As soon as he had the vision, straightway we made efforts to set out for Macedonia, being sure that God had called us to preach the gospel to them" (Acts 16:9-10).

In point of fact, the vision of Patrick meant as much for Ireland as the vision of Paul meant for Macedonia: each carried Christ to a country that knew little of Him. "Come and walk among us once more." Patrick did. And that brings me to my second point: what the vision did for the Ireland that called him.

You see, Patrick has walked among the Irish in two ways: as a missionary and as a saint. As a missionary, he came to a land that was largely pagan, and he left it virtually Christian. In his own

78

words, "those who never had a knowledge of God, but until now always worshipped idols and things impure, have now been made a people of the Lord, and are called sons of God, . . . the sons and daughters of the kings of the Irish are seen to be monks and virgins of Christ." [6] He poured God's life into untold thousands; untold thousands he anointed with the Spirit of Christ; everywhere he infused new priests with power to change wheat and wine into the body and blood of Christ, sent them forth "to baptize and exhort a people in need and want." [7] And for Ireland he suffered. As Patrick phrased it:

"I know perfectly well . . . that poverty and misfortune become me better than riches and pleasures. For Christ the Lord, too, was poor for our sakes; and I, unhappy wretch that I am, have no wealth even if I wished for it. Daily I expect murder, fraud, or captivity, or whatever it may be; 'but I fear none of these things' (Acts 20:24) because of the promises of heaven. . . . Greatly and exceedingly do I wish . . . that He should give me His chalice to drink, as He gave it also to the others who loved Him. . . . And if ever I have done any

[6] *Confession* 41; tr. Bieler, p. 34.
[7] *Confession* 40; tr. Bieler, p. 33.

good for my God whom I love, I beg Him to grant me that I may shed my blood with those exiles and captives for His name, even though I should be denied a grave, or my body be woefully torn to pieces limb by limb by hounds or wild beasts, or the fowls of the air devour it." [8]

In fact, so intimately did Patrick identify himself with his God-given people that this missionary from Britain could write: ". . . we are Irish." [9]

As a missionary, Patrick *ended* his efforts for Ireland in 461. As a saint, it was in 461 that Patrick *began* his work for Ireland. And the success of his efforts is there for all to see: fifteen hundred years of Irish history. There are shadows, of course; for the blood and sweat, the tears and prayers of Patrick have not washed sin from the face of Ireland. And still it is an isle of saints; still the picture is splendidly Christian and highly heroic. For Patrick has achieved a remarkable result: he has made it the normal thing for a son or daughter of St. Patrick to live the first great commandment in the law and the Gospel—through the bittersweet of Irish history to love God with their

[8] *Confession* 55, 57, 59; tr. Bieler, pp. 38, 39.
[9] *Letter to the Soldiers of Coroticus* 16; tr. Bieler, p. 45.

whole heart, with their whole soul, with their whole mind, and with all their strength.

A son of St. Patrick, a daughter of St. Patrick—this suggests my third point: what the vision of Patrick can do for those who recall it today, for you and me. The American temptation today is to be insular, to be a tight little island. It is an understandable temptation. We have given so much, and we have gotten so little. Missionaries give themselves to Red China, only to be martyred; soldiers give themselves to Vietnam, only to be slaughtered; money goes to Yugoslavia, only to be misspent; a Peace Corps scatters abroad, and is greeted with suspicion. Why not shake off all this ingratitude? We need our priests here, for missions at home; we need our warriors here, for America; we need our atoms here, for peace; we need our money here, for our children.

The temptation is understandable, the reaction justifiable. But I am not speaking of American justice; I am speaking of Christian love. There are two devastating answers to that temptation. The first answer is Patrick. Suppose he had answered the voice of the Irish, the vision in the night: "I will *not* come to you, for you once held me in chains. I will *not* walk among you, for you are pagan, uncivilized, ungrateful. I will *not* help you there in Ireland, for much work must be done here in Britain." Why, there would have been no Columbanus, no Columba, and no Colman; no Finan and no Finnian; there would have been no Iona to evangelize and educate the Isles, no Christian invasion of the Continent. If Patrick had said no to his vision, how many of you would be here today?

The second answer is Ireland, the ancestry of so many Americans; and it is to *these* Americans especially that I speak. The Irish immigrant has never been merely an exile. He has traditionally been a missionary: he has brought to other shores a creed and a culture, a deep faith in God and a rich way of life. It would be tragic indeed if the creed and the culture which your fathers carried to these shores were to be imprisoned here: thus far and no farther! It would mean that St. Patrick is your hero but not your model; that he is a source of pride but not of inspiration; that you have changed the Irish conception of civilization and sanctity from a corporate thing to a selfish commodity, to be wrapped in a green napkin and buried till the Master comes. If your creed and your culture are shackled here and do not escape, if they build

82

only American cities and American cathedrals, if your Celtic heritage does not burst its American chains as Patrick burst the bonds of Roman Britain, I warn you: your creed and your culture may corrupt and die.

A man is not a son of St. Patrick simply because he has a vivid remembrance of oppression, but only if oppression has made him ready to weep for all the oppressed. A man is not a son of St. Patrick simply because he kept his faith in time of crucifixion, but only if he spreads his faith in the day of resurrection. A man is not a son of St. Patrick simply because he hid his culture in the hedge schools of Ireland, but only if he opens his culture to a whole little world. The sons of Patrick have proved over and over that they have his sense of justice; what remains to be proved is that they have his gift of love: love for every human being, love even for their enemies. Otherwise the words of Christ are all too pertinent: "If you love only those who love you, what merit is there in that? For even godless people love those who love them. And if you help only those who help you, what merit is there in that? Even godless people act in that way" (Lk 6:32-33). It would be an ironic aftermath of Patrick if the oppressed

83

become the oppressors, if the slaves become the masters, if the image men have of the Irish in America is that of a people too entrenched to be adventurous, a race that has suffered too much to forgive.

Happily, genuine sons of St. Patrick, and genuine daughters, are very much in evidence. One extraordinary son should be an inspiration to you. Looking on a poor young peasant in a coolie suit hoeing a rice field, he wrote these lyric lines: "I choose you and with you countless millions of God's children like you: men white, black, and brown; souls impoverished and unendowed. I choose you and I dedicate myself to you, and I ask no other privilege but to devote the energies of my soul to such as you. You are my father and my mother, my sister and my brother. Men of no attraction, you attract me. Souls of no distinction, you dazzle me. Clodhoppers of the world, you claim me."

The son of St. Patrick who wrote those words was born in Cumberland, Maryland. The last foreign missionary in Red China, Bishop James Edward Walsh will end his days in a Communist prison.

Am I asking you to be a missionary? Why, of course. The St. Patrick parade that transforms a city into an emerald isle should not be a march of triumph, a conqueror's strut. Each footfall—up Fifth Avenue in New York, down Cathedral Street in Baltimore, the length and breadth of the nation—each footfall should be a memory and a promise. Each footfall should be a remembrance of things past, of the culture that has touched America's streets—touched them with Irish tears and laughter, with Irish wit and eloquence, with Irish courage and intelligence, with Irish devotion to God and man—touched them at times with human sinfulness, with the weakness that corrodes and the power that corrupts. And each footfall should be a promise, a dedication to the future. For yours too is a vision in the night, the voice of strangers—strangers on your street or strangers in the Congo—to the Patricks of America: "Come and walk among us. Come with your Christ, to light up our darkness. Come with your culture, to refine our crudeness. Come with your compassion, to stir new hope from our ashes. Walk among us, with your wealth if you will, with your weapons if you must, but always with your love. Come and walk among us."

st. thomas aquinas
sanctity and intelligence

N THE history of Christian intellectualism, few names rival Thomas Aquinas. Here is a man whose breath of life was the mind, whose ceaseless search was for truth. Here is a man who, as Chesterton put it, "loved books and lived on books . . . lived the very life of the clerk or scholar in *The Canterbury Tales,* who would rather have a hundred books of Aristotle and his philosophy than any wealth the world could give him." [1] A man whose lifework rested on the thesis that reason can be trusted. A man who saw that truth is everywhere, that wisdom cries in the streets. A man who had no fear of truth, who had to fight for his own approach to truth. A man who begged with tears not to be made a bishop, for his consuming passion was the life of the mind.

[1] G. K. Chesterton, *St. Thomas Aquinas* (New York: Sheed & Ward, 1933), p. 4.

This is the man who, in thirty Dominican years, wrote more than sixty works. The man who confessed that, after God, his greatest grace was: "I have understood everything I ever read." The man who, over eight long years, fused revelation and reason, the word of God and the work of man, into an unparalleled unity, a heady synthesis that reveals God in His secret life, man as he comes forth from God, man as he returns to God through Christ. This is the man who heard from the crucified Christ: "You have written well of me; what reward will you have?" and answered: "Nothing, Lord, save you." The man who, three months before his death, put down his pen forever with the sigh: "I can do no more. Such secrets have been revealed to me that all I have written seems now of little value."

And this is the man who cast his theology in song—in hymns that are a happy marriage of mind and heart, of truth and love, of intellect and piety, of doctrine and devotion. For this is the man who first murmured *Pange lingua*, "Sing, my tongue, the mystery"; the first to hymn *Lauda Sion*, "Laud, O Sion, thy Salvation."

How did Thomas explain his own paradox? How did he justify this wedding of syllogism and song, of philosophy and poetry, of knowledge and love? In this remarkable paragraph: "There are two ways of desiring knowledge. One way is to desire it as a perfection of one's self; and that is the way philosophers desire it. The other way is to desire it not as a perfection of one's self but because through this knowledge the one we love becomes present to us; and that is the way saints desire it."

And that is the twin burden of my message here. There are two ways of desiring knowledge. Each is good, but one is better. One makes for learning, the other for sanctity. One ends in sheer knowledge, the other in intelligent love.

"One way of desiring knowledge," Aquinas affirms, "is to desire it as a perfection of one's self." In the Christian tradition, intelligence has always been held in reverence. For the God-given function of the human mind is to know. As the eye is made to see and the ear to hear, as the hand is shaped to touch and the heart to love, so your mind is fashioned by God to know.

It is a good thing, then, that the mind of a human being—that power which sets you high above the animal and a bit below the angel—comes in contact with truth and reality, with all that is human, with so much that is divine.

89

This mind looks into a microscope and is filled with the wonder of life which the naked eye cannot see. This mind speeds over oceans more swiftly than the jet and touches human beings from Siberia to Saigon, from Algeria to East Germany. This mind flees back into the past and rediscovers a universe that is perhaps five billion years old, rediscovers an America four centuries young. This mind plucks meaning from the strings of a harp and the whisper of the wind, from a sonnet or a sonata, from Michelangelo's Moses and the Mona Lisa. This mind looks into the minds of philosophers from ancient Greece to modern France, from Plato's world of ideas to the existentialism of Sartre, to share their tortured search for what is real, for what is true. This mind looks into the mind of God as it reveals itself in creation, on a cross, and in the lines of His own book; for the man of broad knowledge, the man of wisdom, echoes the remarkable passage in the Book of Jeremiah:

Thus says the Lord:
"Let not the wise man boast of his wisdom,
Nor the strong man boast of his strength,
Nor the rich man boast of his riches!
But if one must boast, let him boast of this,
That he knows and understands me."

(Jer 9:23-24)

90

The result should be revolutionary indeed. Not that now you know everything; only the incurably ignorant claim omniscience. But you have learned that reality, truth, is a many-splendored thing, as deep and as boundless as the God who *is* Reality, who *is* Truth; that there are different ways of reaching reality, of achieving truth; that the scientist and the poet, the psychologist and the artist, the sociologist and the historian, the philosopher and the theologian, each has his place in this endless quest. You have seen *what* each is trying to do, and you have glimpsed *how* each does it.

It is then that you see science not as a godless thing, a suspect thing, the factory of war, but as man's response to God's command "Master the earth," man's effort to discover in nature what nature's God has hidden there. It is then that you see the arts not as a luxury, but as a human yearning to imprison truth and beauty, not in a definition but in symbol or syllable or symphony, to capture love and sacrifice, majestic serenity and elusive loveliness, life and death, not in a formula but full-blooded, thrilling through pen and brush and marble. It is then that you see philosophy not as a game, mental gymnastics, badminton with words, but

91

as the supreme effort of human reason to explain man and his universe. Then you see revelation and religion not as a crutch for the weak, not as a power machine with Ten Commandments and an Index of Forbidden Books, but as God breaking through history and man responding to God in love. Then you see history itself as more than a set of blind dates, begin to appreciate Santayana's warning: "Those who learn nothing from the past are doomed to repeat it."

This is intelligence: to grasp what the human mind is made for—knowledge; to glimpse how the human mind achieves knowledge on its varied levels; and, above all, a consuming thirst throughout life, a racking yearning to know, to understand.

All this is good, for it perfects man's mind; it makes him more of a man, more human; it makes him more like the God who *is* Mind, who *is* Intelligence. But for a Christian, for a religious man or woman, this is not enough. For a religious man or woman, as St. Thomas suggests, knowledge dares not remain sterile. "The other way of desiring knowledge is to desire it not as a perfection of one's self but because through this knowledge the one we love be-

92

comes present to us; and that is the way saints desire it."

Through knowledge the one we love becomes present to us. This is true even on a sheerly natural level, even divorced from God. It is a touching thing to see the love of man and maid unfold like a flower; to see knowledge deepen their love, love quicken their knowledge; to see how understanding destroys distance, brings a loved one to life in a room he has walked or a way he has talked, in a cheek he has caressed or a child he has fathered. Even when absent, he is present; and the deeper her knowledge, the more pervasive his presence. Knowledge leads to love, and love perfects knowledge.

This is even more true on the level of the religious, on the level of the divine. For a religious man or woman, for one who believes in God, knowledge is not sterile if it makes what you love present to you. And what you love as a child of God ought to have three dimensions: things, people, and God.

First, things. In the Christian vision of the universe, things are, in a genuine sense, holy. For all this was born of God. Each flower, each cloud, each mountain range goes back in time to some nameless, perhaps shapeless, certainly mysterious matter that is significant for one unforgettable reason: it was fashioned by God. More than that: earth, sea, and sky are God's struggle to paint His features on the canvas of a world, so that the visible images the Invisible —a whirlwind reflects His power, a mountain mirrors His majesty, surging waves His irresistibleness, a star-flecked sky His breath-taking loveliness. That is why the discovery of God's universe through history and literature, through science and art, should draw you into closer intimacy with every work of His hands, however mute, however brute. It should lend you the love of Julian, an English mystic in the days of Chaucer. In movingly simple language she wrote:

"[Our good Lord] shewed [me] a little thing, the size of a hazelnut, which seemed to lie in the palm of my hand; and it was as round as any ball. I looked upon it with the eye of my understanding, and thought, 'What may this be?' I was answered in a general way, thus: 'It is all that is made.' I wondered how long it could last; for it seemed as though it might suddenly fade away to nothing, it was so small. And I was answered in my understanding: 'It lasts, and ever shall last; for God loveth it. And even so hath everything being—by the love of God.'

"In this little thing I saw three properties. The first is that God made it; the second, that God loveth it; the third, that God keepeth it. . . ." [2]

Second, people. Through poet and painter, through newsman and novelist, through psychologist and sociologist, through direct experience, you have seen living man—man with his frailty and his strength, his virtues and his vices, his pride and his passion, his tragic greatness. But this is a sterile knowledge, a godless knowledge, this knowledge is not Christian, unless compassion is born of it, and love. Love because, like you, these human beings are like God: in their twin power, in their power to know and to love, they have been shaped to God's image, they share in their fragile way His infinity, His perfection. Love because, in the Christian vision, each of these men and women is linked to Christ by the arms of His cross. Not just some, but all; not just the clean and the white and the prosperous and the God-fearing, but the dirty and repulsive, the black and brown and yellow, the poor and hungry and blind and lame and drunk

[2] *The Revelations of Divine Love of Julian of Norwich;* trans. James Walsh, S.J. (London: Burns, Oates & Washbourne, Ltd., 1961), p. 53.

and bewildered, even the man who says in his heart "There is no God."

There is one kind of knowledge that makes the mass of men an object: there it is, out there, to be pitied or censured, to be helped or rebuffed, to be answered or ignored. And there is another kind of knowledge that makes every human being part of me: here he is, in here, to be understood and loved, in harmony with the Roman poet, "Nothing that is human is a stranger to me"—in harmony with the command of Christ, "Love one another as I have loved you" (Jn 15:12).

And finally there is God Himself. It is not enough to know Him. In the long course of history many human beings have known Him: philosophers and philanderers, criminals and Christmas Christians—even Judas. There are men and women who can prove that God exists; there are countless creatures for whom God *is*. But all too often He exists as someone or something out there, someone I think about as I might think about Napoleon or Nehru, about John Kennedy or John XXIII. Rarely as someone here, whom I love, whom knowledge makes present with a thrill that only lover and beloved experience.

Love of God makes a significant dif-

97

ference. It is then you see that "the world is charged with the grandeur of God." [3] It is then that all creation, from the neutrino to outer space, speaks to you of its Creator. It is then that God becomes for you the God of whom Scripture speaks: a living God, in the here-and-now of history, God with you, acting for your salvation, faithful to His promises, a loving God who demands from man a response of love. Not simply a God who is all-powerful, but a God imprisoned in flesh; not merely a God who comes alive through the things He has made, but a God from whose eyes tears drop, from whose lips a smile is born; not only a God who gave you life, but a God who gave His life for you.

The point I am making is at once simple and profound. In no phase of human living will your knowledge be thoroughly human, nowhere will it be authentically Christian, unless it is impregnated with love: love for God's creation, for God's people, for God Himself. Cold knowledge of nature's forces, without reverence for the work of God's hands, risks making each atom a peril-

[3] Gerard Manley Hopkins, "God's Grandeur," in *Poems of Gerard Manley Hopkins,* 2nd ed., Robert Bridges, ed. (London: Oxford University Press, 1930), p. 26.

ous, destructive thing. Sheer knowledge, empty of love, can only turn a marriage barren. Unless you love, the poor will never forgive you for the bread you offer them. And all your discovery of God—whether it be a rose that reveals Him, or the Son of Mary—will end in frustration if it does not end in oneness, in a person-to-person relationship between a human being and a living God.

This, as St. Thomas saw it and lived it, this is the knowledge that makes saints. It escapes the skeptic, who searches but does not expect to find; and it escapes that Christian who refuses to search because there is nothing more to find. In the Christian scheme of things, learning is not a luxury, and ignorance is not a virtue. Not that naked knowledge will ever save. But knowledge is a first step to love; discovery can deepen love; and, in God's plan, all your earth-bound discoveries are intimations of immortality, are to end in that eternal, ecstatic discovery which is the knowledge of your God face to face, and that ceaseless life of intelligent love which is eternal life—loving Him who *is* your Life.

st. peter canisius
sanctity and education

HUMAN GREATNESS is born of crisis. There is a challenge and a response. There is a need, earth-shaking or soul-shattering, and the need is met.

At times the crisis is primarily interior. I am thinking of Augustine as we have seen him—Augustine sin-scarred and tear-laden, tormented with exquisite anguish because the fever of the flesh burns him and he dares only pray: "Lord, give me chastity, but not yet." A voice commands him: "Take up and read." He takes up the New Testament; his eyes fall on Paul: "Not in revelry and drunkenness, not in debauchery and wantonness, not in strife and jealousy; but put on the Lord Jesus Christ, and as for the flesh, take no thought for its lusts." And

This chapter first appeared under the title, "The Vision of Peter Canisius," *Catholic Mind*, 55, No. 1129 (Jan.-Feb., 1957), 49-55.

Augustine tells us: "I had no wish to read further, and no need. For in that instant . . . it was as though a light of utter confidence shone in all my heart, and all the darkness of uncertainty vanished away." [2] At that moment a saint was born.

At times the crisis is primarily external. I am thinking of June 4, 1940. Poland lay prostrate, and Finland had fallen. Norway had been crushed beneath the Nazi heel, and Denmark had surrendered without a struggle. The Dutch army had been beaten in the field, and the Belgian had capitulated. In ten days Paris would be occupied, and from an unforgettable port called Dunkirk 335,000 French and British troops had been miraculously evacuated. On that spring day a man of sixty-six rose in the House of Commons—a man who could offer his country "nothing . . . but blood, toil, tears, and sweat"—and said:

"We shall go on to the end, we shall fight in France, we shall fight on the seas and oceans, we shall fight with growing confidence and growing strength in the air, we shall defend our Island, whatever the cost may be, we shall fight

[2] St. Augustine, *Confessions* 8, 12; tr. Sheed, p. 179. For a more detailed account of this crisis, see pp. 40-41.

on the beaches, we shall fight on the
landing grounds, we shall fight in the
fields and in the streets, we shall fight
in the hills; we shall never surrender,
and even if, which I do not for a moment believe, this Island or a large part
of it were subjugated and starving,
then our Empire beyond the seas . . .
would carry on the struggle, until, in
God's good time, the New World, with
all its power and might, steps forth to
the rescue and the liberation of the
old." [3]

At that moment a nation was reborn.

Human greatness attaches to Peter
Canisius. As with Augustine and Churchill, so too with Canisius, greatness was
born of crisis. There was a challenge
and he responded to it. There was a
need, earth-shaking *and* soul-shattering,
and he met it.

The crisis? Some might call it the
Reformation. When Canisius arrived in
"Catholic" Bavaria, nine out of every
ten Germans had been lost to Catholicism. When he reached "Catholic"
Vienna, not a single priest had been
ordained in Vienna in twenty years.
When he reached "Catholic" Cracow,
he found 10,000 Poles hurrying forth

[3] Winston S. Churchill, *Blood, Sweat, and Tears*
(New York: G. P. Putnam's Sons, 1941), p. 297.

on feast days to listen to a Lutheran sermon.[4]

For Canisius, however, the Reformation was a *result;* his eyes, like ours, were fixed on the *root* of the Reformation. I am not concerned at the moment with the plight of the priesthood. On that score the tragic evidence is there for all to read. We know from a faithful eyewitness that the clergy of Bavaria led "such lazy, gluttonous, drunken, dissolute, gambling lives as to be a scandal before God and the world."[5] We know that numbers of priests could not have passed the most elementary test in Christian doctrine. We know that most of the priests in Ingolstadt never said a word of the breviary on the plea that it was too long and too difficult. We know that the clergy of the Vienna Cathedral had to be ordered by the government to hear confessions at Easter time.[6] Is it any wonder that Peter Canisius, in a sermon of 1564, pronounced this damning indictment on the clergy of Augsburg: "With them there is no honesty at home, no sobriety

[4] Cf. J. Brodrick, S.J., *Saint Peter Canisius, S.J., 1521–1597* (London: Sheed & Ward, 1935), pp. 131, 170-71, 373-74.

[5] The witness was a contemporary of Canisius, Dr. Martin Eisengrein, who strove mightily for a genuine Catholic reformation; cf. Brodrick, *op. cit.,* p. 131.

[6] Cf. Brodrick, pp. 132, 156, 194-95.

at table, no continence in bed, no study in books, no devotion in heart or soul . . ."? [7]

All that is true, and more. But what concerns me now is what concerned Canisius then: the ignorance of the Catholic people. From the pulpit the Catholic masses of Austria heard too little of the Catholic substance, of Catholic doctrine, of Catholic devotion. In consequence, as Father Brodrick puts it, Canisius was confronted with conditions "which threatened the swift extinction in Austria of all that he held dearest." [8] And in the university the Catholic intellectual—the man with a large love of wisdom and a deep devotion to Wisdom Incarnate—was nonexistent. He had died from hairsplitting in the field of philosophy; he had died of slow starvation in Scripture and theology. "In this university," Canisius wrote of Ingolstadt, "it is almost a convention that students need not trouble to study letters, least of all sacred letters." [9]

Therein lay the challenge to Catholicism: not so much impiety as ignorance, not so much bad wills as uninstructed minds. And the crisis was genuine, the

[7] Brodrick, p. 588.
[8] Brodrick, p. 211.
[9] Brodrick, p. 143.

peril was real. For, if the tragedy of a human will is its divorce from what is good, the tragedy of a human mind is its separation from what is true.

What was Canisius' response? A catechism and a college. The catechism (really three catechisms, for three stages of youthful ignorance) was a remarkable achievement on several counts. In the first place, it is inescapable proof of what Cardinal Faulhaber remarked thirty years ago: "The most Canisian thing about Canisius was his love for youth." Secondly, it was the only Catholic catechism that could compete, in lucidity and conciseness, with Luther's catechism, a best seller that saw one hundred thousand copies in circulation in forty years. Thirdly, much of it breathes a tenderness and an affection that echo Tauler, Suso, and St. Gertrude. Before Canisius died, his catechisms were circulating in fifteen languages, had been re-edited or reprinted more than two hundred times. Eighteen years after his death his first biographer wrote: "Canisius is beginning to speak in the tongues of all peoples, in German, Slav, Italian, Spanish, Polish, Greek, Czech, English, Scots, Ethiopian, . . . Hindustani and Japanese, so that nowadays he may fairly be accounted the teacher of practically every nation." The children, he knew, were the Church of tomorrow: "Win them," he reasoned, "and the world is won." One of his last actions on earth, at seventy-five, was to edit the Shortest Catechism with the words divided into syllables, "to enable my dear little children to learn it more easily." Little wonder that, as late as 1925, in some districts of Germany parents could still be heard asking their children: "Have you learned your Canisius?" [10]

The second significant answer: a college. I do not mean his exalted rank as Rector of the University of Ingolstadt. That thankless task Canisius summed up in a single expressive sentence: "The Rector's principal duties are to register the names of new students, to compel debtors to pay their dues, to hear the complaints which citizens and women bring against the young men, to arrest, reprimand, and imprison undergraduates who get drunk or roam about the town at night, and, finally, to preside at festive gatherings, academic meetings, and functions connected with the conferring of degrees." [11] If you would see the type of distraction that dulled this hammer of heretics for months at a

[10] On Canisius' catechisms, cf. Brodrick, pp. 221-52.

[11] Brodrick, pp. 154-55.

107

time and slowed the Counter Reformation to a walk, read his prohibition against students carrying stones and knives: school "is not a military camp but a temple of the Muses." [12] Or listen to Peter's proclamation to the flower of Ingolstadt:

"We are informed that certain students wander about the streets in gangs, barbarously and wickedly exploding *bombardae* [muskets], not only during the day but at night when Almighty God wishes every living thing on earth to be quiet. Others disturb the citizens by blowing trumpets and behaving like complete lunatics. By these presents we strictly prohibit such scandals, and recall to your memory the statute against *bombardae,* which we now declare valid and operative in perpetuity." [13]

It is not *bombardae* I have in mind; that is a rector's cross. The significant thing is this: Canisius founded or helped to found eighteen colleges. The place names sound like a litany of the glory that was Europe: Cologne, Vienna, Prague, Ingolstadt, Strasbourg, Trier, Freiburg im Breisgau, Zabern, Dillingen, Munich, Würzburg, Hall in Tirol, Speyer, Innsbruck, Landshut, Lands-

[12] Brodrick, p. 299.
[13] Brodrick, p. 158.

berg, Molsheim in Alsace, and Fribourg in Switzerland. The figures are impressive; more impressive still is Canisius' vision. A Catholic college, as he saw it, had a twin exigency: it had to be a college, and it had to be Catholic. It had to be a *college*—a center of genuine intellectual effort, a place where a human being could learn. In his college this world's wisdom would be found—all that is summed up in the idea "liberal arts." And in his college would be found the new methods in theological study introduced by humanism—that is, intelligent investigation of Christian sources. This is why his intellectual credo contains one of the most startling sentences he ever uttered: "Better a college without a church of its own than a college without a library of its own." [14]

But a Canisius college was to be a *Catholic* college: it would fail ingloriously of its function if it did not stimulate a deeper penetration into the mystery that is God, a more profound realization of the newness of life that was born when the Son of God stepped down from heaven and put on not merely our dress but our flesh. What the Continent needed was a Catholic

[14] Brodrick, p. 186.

life that fed not on superstition but on mystery, and not so much on mystery as on understanding of mystery. What Europe needed was intelligent sanctity and sanctified intelligence. The vision of Canisius was rarely more evident than when he wrote: "Sincerity of life wedded to sacred learning is an attractive combination, and piety conjoined with discernible wisdom easily makes disciples. Truth rejoices to have its claims made good by word and example, and once vindicated it draws men, even against their will, to worship it, love it and follow its leading." [15] And for a remarkable insight into the relationship between knowledge and love, the impact of heart on mind, I submit the wisdom of Canisius: "Where do studies thrive best . . . ? Is it not in those places where the practice of frequent Communion flourishes?" [16]

Two aspects of this intellectual enterprise are all but unbelievable: its crown and its cross. It is a success story, yes— from the college at Cologne with a thousand scholars at his death, through the college at Prague that vitalized Bohemia's faith, to the college at Fribourg that has made Canisius a symbol and inspiration of Catholic intellectual-

[15] Brodrick, pp. 149-50.
[16] Brodrick, p. 78.

ism in Switzerland. When Canisius invaded Germany in 1550, it was with two companions; when he left it thirty years later, 1111 Jesuits were at work in the Empire.

But the crown was hard won—was won, in fact, from a cross. There were small nuisances: the Croatian nobleman who tried to prove by geometry that there must be three natures in Christ; the Superior who crammed an Italian cuisine into the reluctant maws of his Austrian brethren; even the problem of supplying a beverage for an ill-fed faculty. (In this connection Father Brodrick remarks that the beer with which the Upper German Province had to be content was of the kind known to certain Devonshire workmen as "Just Right." One of them, being asked to explain the name, answered: "It's this way. If it were any better we wouldn't get it, and if it were any worse we couldn't drink it. So it's just right." [17]) But there was genuine crucifixion too—from the sword of sorrow that pierced his soul in nominally Catholic Bavaria to the Zwinglian mud and snowballs and rotten turnips that bespattered his body in Bern. His reaction? "May God turn the snowballs into a good foun-

[17] Brodrick, p. 288, note 2.

111

dation for the college of Fribourg!" [18] God did. It is but another proof, if proof be needed, that human greatness can be purchased only with "blood, toil, tears, and sweat."

Today, as in Canisius' day, a crisis confronts us. Not, indeed, the spectacle of a Europe forsaking Catholicism for Protestantism; rather, as Pius XI put it, "a world that in large part has almost fallen back into paganism." [19] Whatever may be shaping contemporary culture, it is not Christianity. On the academic level the air we breathe is naturalistic. What dare we no longer believe? The proclamation of John Dewey still rings loud and clear: "Faith in the divine author and authority in which Western civilization confided— and inherited ideas of the soul and its destiny—have been made impossible for the cultivated mind of the Western world." [20] What must we believe? The credo of Bertrand Russell is still atheist dogma: "That Man is the product of causes which had no prevision of the

[18] Brodrick, pp. 774-75.
[19] Pius XI, Encyclical *Quadragesimo anno;* translation from *Two Basic Social Encyclicals* (New York: Benziger Bros., Inc., 1943), p. 187.
[20] Quoted from Louis J. A. Mercier, "American Education Must Right about Face," *The Catholic Mind through Fifty Years, 1903–1953* (New York: American Press, n.d.), p. 202.

112

end they were achieving; that his origin, his growth, his hopes and fears, his loves and beliefs, are but the outcome of accidental collocations of atoms; that no fire, no heroism, no intensity of thought and feeling can preserve an individual life beyond the grave; that all the labours of the ages, all the devotion, all the inspiration, all the noonday brightness of human genius, are destined to extinction in the vast death of the solar system, and that the whole temple of Man's achievement must inevitably be buried beneath the debris of a universe in ruins—all these things, if not quite beyond dispute, are yet so nearly certain, that no philosophy which rejects them can hope to stand." [21]

There, in brief compass, lies the crisis; there is your challenge. What will your response be? There is the need, earth-shaking and soul-shattering. How will you meet it? Basically, as Canisius met the crisis that confronted him: through intelligent sanctity and sanctified intelligence. Your crisis of the moment is intellectual, and it is Catholic; knowledge is the issue, and faith. It is an age-old problem, come to rest restlessly in you: *fides quaerens intellectum*—faith,

[21] Bertrand Russell, *Philosophical Essays* (London and New York: Longmans, Green & Co., Inc., 1910), p. 60.

113

belief, in search of understanding, intelligence, insight. But conversely, too, *intellectus quaerens fidem*—intelligence in search of faith.

The alternative that faces today's Catholic was phrased with harsh simplicity by E. I. Watkin in a chapter heading of his book *The Catholic Centre*. The chapter is entitled "Come in or Go out." [22] For the educated Catholic in the contemporary crisis there is no room on the periphery of Catholicism. The catechism is inadequate, because dry bones will never give life—to the world or to yourself. Emotion is not enough, because emotion is fickle and will not abide. You must give to your faith what the Son of God insisted you give to your love: you must give not merely your whole heart but your whole mind as well.

Concretely, I dare each one of you to do two things. In the first place, I dare you, who believe, to search for intelligence. I challenge you to catch a glimpse of the Trinity, not as a most ingenious paradox, but as a mystery of love, the model-without-beginning for every love that has ever begun. I challenge you to see in creation not primarily a production from nothing, but God

[22] E. I. Watkin, *The Catholic Centre* (New York: Sheed & Ward, 1939), p. 49.

painting His portrait on the canvas of a world: to see that earth, sea, and sky reflect His glory, that there is no white-cap, no star, no peony that does not speak of Him. I dare you to discover in redemption not simply a harrowing price paid to a just God, but the vision of St. John: "God so loved the world. . . ." I challenge you to study the Church not as an organization with laws and penalties, but as an organism, a body, the continuation of Christ through the ages. I dare you to grasp the reality of grace, not as something airy and unsubstantial, but as the life of God coursing through you like another bloodstream. I dare you to penetrate the meaning of four simple words, "This is my body," until you fall on your knees and whisper with Thomas Aquinas:

See, Lord, at thy service low lies here a heart
Lost, all lost in wonder at the God thou art.[23]

These, and a hundred depths more, I dare you to plumb, because this is faith in search of insight.

In the second place, I dare you to do all this in the context of a genuine, a

[23] St. Thomas Aquinas, Hymn "Adoro te"; trans. Gerard Manley Hopkins, in Robert Bridges and W. H. Gardner, *Poems of Gerard Manley Hopkins*, 3rd ed. (London: Oxford University Press, 1948), p. 186.

loving faith. Actually, I am asking you to test the influence of love on understanding, by loving God with your whole heart, your whole soul, your whole mind, and all your strength; and by loving every human being as Christ our Lord has loved you. I am asking you simply to verify the dictum of Peter Canisius: "Where do studies thrive best? Where frequent Communion flourishes." This I dare you to do, because this is intelligence in search of faith.

For every Catholic intellectual who achieves this ideal, a saint will be born. If enough Catholic intellectuals achieve it, a nation may well be reborn.

st. christopher
sanctity and selflessness

I N A thirteenth-century manual of piety called *The Golden Legend* there is an engaging story of a pagan named Reprobus. Reprobus was a giant in stature, and it was his resolve to seek out and to serve the most powerful prince in the world. He thought he had found him in a king of high renown; but it turned out that this king was not all-powerful: he was afraid of the devil. So Reprobus sought out the devil; he thought he had found him in a knight cruel and horrible; but it turned out that this devil was not all-powerful: he was afraid of a cross erected on a highway—afraid because a man called Christ had hung on that cross. And so Reprobus went on to seek out this Christ. Along the way a hermit in a desert taught him Christianity and told him that, if he wanted Christ to show Himself, he must do a service for Christ: strong giant that he was, he must lodge by a river and carry over the river all who might wish to cross. And this he did, with a great pole in his hand, many days, all manner of people, without ceasing.

One night, as he slept in his lodge, a child awakened him: "Come out and carry me over." He lifted the child on his shoulders, took up his pole, and entered the water. But the water rose, and the child was heavy as lead, grew heavier and heavier, till the giant was in anguish and afraid they would drown. On the other side he put the child aground and gasped: "Child, you have put me in great peril. Your weight was as if I had all the world on my shoulders. No greater burden could I bear." The child answered: "Christopher, do not be amazed. You have borne on your shoulders not only the world, but Him who created the world. I am Jesus Christ, the King whom you serve in this work." [1]

Such is the famous legend of St. Christopher, "Christ-bearer." The unbeliever looks at the story, weighs the evidence, and concludes: It never hap-

[1] Alban Butler, *The Lives of the Saints* 7, rev. by Herbert Thurston, S.J., and Donald Attwater (London: Burns, Oates & Washbourne, 1932), 358-64.

pened. The Christian looks at the story, meditates on it, and concludes: Did it happen? It doesn't much matter. For, whether it happened or not, this story reveals a widespread Christian conviction, a perennial Christian truth. A twin truth: It is the task of a Christian to bear his brother's burden; and in bearing his brother, the Christian is carrying Christ.

It is the task of a Christian to bear his brother's burden. A Christian peril today is the pagan peril of every day: selfishness. It is an insidious danger. On the one hand, there is a selfishness which is sinless, inescapable, even Christian. I am speaking of the selfishness which means no more than that you are concerned about yourself, about *your* dear ones, about *your* God. I mean the sinless self-love where you love yourself as much as you love others. I mean the inescapable self-love where you take high care of yourself and yours: feed your body, sanctify your soul, beautify your home, increase your possessions, slave for those who are one flesh with you. I mean the Christian self-love where you struggle to find in God, now and forever, *your* joy, *your* happiness.

All that is good and it can be Christian. What is perilous is another kind of selfishness, a selfishness which is un-

christian. I mean a concern with yourself and yours to the exclusion of your
fellow man. Where you limit your love
and your self-giving to your own country, your own city, your own community,
your own creed, your own color, your
own circle.

The reasons are basically two: either
you have no *use* for the rest of men or
you have no *time* for them. Some human
beings have no use for anyone outside
their own charmed circle. "India is lazy
and Italy is dirty, the Russians are bar-
barians and the Spaniards are fascists,
the Germans are power-hungry and the
Scandinavians are sex-crazy, the Egyp-
tians are a menace to the Middle East
and the English are oppressors of the
Irish, the Puerto Ricans are juvenile and
senile delinquents, the Cubans are ungrateful—and all of them want our
money."

But most good people simple have
no time for the rest of humanity. The
past is for them a tragic memory of
wasted blood and fruitless giving; the
future is ominous mystery. Only the
present is real—*my* present. Selma and
Katanga, East and West Germany, Russia and her satellites, labor and manage-
ment, overpopulation and unemploy-
ment, poverty and cancer, even the
human beings on my own street—their

120

problems are so vast, so complicated, and I am so helpless, so ignorant. I have so much of my own work to do, and I have so little time.

That is a very human reaction; but it is no more than human. The Christian approach is far different. The Christian maxim is the command of St. Paul: "Bear one another's burdens" (Gal 6:2). Not simply the burdens that Paul was stressing when he wrote to the Galatians: Bear with one another's *failings*, one another's *sins*. The burdens you must bear are far broader. They are the misfortunes of a world, and they demand from a Christian a threefold response, a response of head and heart and hand.

First, you must be keenly aware of others' burdens. It is unchristian to play the ostrich, to hide your face from the misery and anguish of human living because it makes you sad or uncomfortable. At this moment, in lovely Lima, thousands of human beings are literally living on the city's garbage dump, because here is their only food. At this moment, hundreds of thousands of Europeans and millions in the Far East are homeless, refugees, because like Joseph and Mary and little Jesus they have fled from the face of a Herod. At this moment, concentration camps dot the face of the earth. At this moment,

there are corpses without graves, dis-
eased without doctors, innocents without freedom. At this moment, in this
fair land, there are hands without work,
stomachs without food, human beings
without human rights. And there are
always the lonely and the loveless, the
aged and the motherless. These burdens
and a thousand more, from Appalachia
to Leningrad, you should be aware of;
these you must face.

Second, heart must follow head. It is
not enough for a true Christian to
know that misery and injustice exist. In
a Christian heart, what is born of this
knowledge is compassion; I "suffer with"
all who suffer. Of course, compassion
cannot mean that I so take to myself
the heartache of a world or an individual that my energy is squandered in
sheer suffering. But compassion does
mean that I am never completely comfortable as long as one brother or sister
cries in vain for bread or justice or love.
Compassion does mean that I tear from
my lips those horrible half-truths, "Charity begins at home," "Let the shiftless
shift for themselves," "They are only
getting what they deserve," "If I give
them an inch, they will take a mile,"
"Why should I give to others what has
cost me sweat and blood and tears to
achieve?" Compassion means that I can

123

weep for the tears of a stranger. In fact, compassion means that no human being is a stranger.

Third, knowledge and compassion should issue in action. Not that your activity will drive hunger and war, disease and injustice, from the face of the earth. It will not; that is not your vocation. But it is your vocation to "love your enemies, do good to those who hate you, and pray for those who persecute and calumniate you" (Mt 5:44). It may well be your vocation to give bread to one faceless refugee, to draw a wan smile from one orphan's lips, to give hope to one disillusioned heart. It is your vocation to impregnate your little acre with a love that is catholic because it embraces every human being who lives and breathes therein.

Yes, your task is to bear your brother's burden, as God gives you to see it and as God gives you to bear it. Head, heart, and hand; knowledge, compassion, and action. The burden is heavy indeed: "as if I had all the world on my shoulders." It can be softened only by the lesson of Christopher: in bearing his brother, the Christian is carrying Christ: "I am Jesus Christ, the King whom you serve in this work."

Do you recall the story of St. Paul? Before his conversion he hated Christians with a murderous hatred. But on his way to Damascus with power to enchain them, a light from heaven flashed around him; he fell to the ground; and he heard a voice asking: "Why do you persecute me?" "Who are you?" he asked. The voice answered: "I am Jesus, whom you are persecuting" (Acts 9:3-5). So intimate is the link between Christ the Head and the Christians who form His Body that, on God's word, to persecute a Christian is to persecute Christ. And conversely, for our comfort, to love a Christian is to love Christ, to bear a Christian on our back is to carry Christ, to be a Christopher. For on the Day of Judgment the King will say to those on His right hand: "Come, blessed of my Father . . . ; for I was hungry, and you gave me food; I was thirsty, and you gave me drink; I was a stranger, and you brought me to your homes; I was naked, and you clothed me; sick, and you took care of me; in prison, and you came to see me. . . . [For] in so far as you did it to one of these, the least of my brethren, you did it to me" (Mt 25:34-40).

And even those who are not part of Christ's Body are still linked to Him by the arms of the cross: He died for every human being, even for the thief who kept cursing Him. What you do

for them, do for Him, and the burden
on your back will say to you as He said
to Christopher: "I am Jesus Christ, the
King whom you serve in this work."

In a remarkable poem, Anne Morrow
Lindbergh has captured the meaning of
St. Christopher for our age. The poem is
entitled *Saint for Our Time* and it runs
like this:

Christopher, come back to earth again.
There is no age in history when men
So cried for you, Saint of a midnight wild,
Who stood beside a stream and heard a child.
Not even Francis, brother to the poor,
Who, barefoot, begged for alms from door to
    door,
And pity-tortured kissed the leper's brow—
Not even Francis is so needed now
As you, Christ-bearer.

                      Christopher, we die
Not for lack of charity; we lie
Imprisoned in our sepulchers of stone,
Wanting your gift, O Saint, your gift alone.
No one will take the burden of the whole
Upon his shoulders; each man in his soul
Thinks his particular grief too great to bear
Without demanding still another's share.

But you—you chose to bear a brother's load
And every man who travelled down your road
You ferried on your back across the flood
Until one night beside the stream there stood,
Wrapped in a cloak of storm, a child who cried
And begged safe passage to the other side—
A child who weighed upon your back like lead,

126

Like earth upon the shoulders of the dead—
And, struggling to the bank while torrents
   whirled,
You found that on your shoulder leaned a
   world.

No wonder that the burden was so great:
You carried in your arms the monstrous weight
Of all men's happiness and all men's pain,
And all men's sorrows on your back had lain.
Even their sins you carried as your own—
Even their sins, you, Christopher, alone!

But who today will take the risk or blame
For someone else? Everyone is the same,
Dreading his neighbor's tongue or pen or deed.
Imprisoned in fear we stand and do not heed
The cry that you once heard across the stream.
"There is no cry," we say, "it is a dream."

Christopher, the waters rise again,
As on that night, the waters rise; the rain
Bites like a whip across a prisoner's back;
The lightning strikes like fighters in attack;
And thunder, like a time-bomb, detonates
The starless sky no searchlight penetrates.

The child is crying on the further shore:
Christopher, come back to earth once more.[2]

[2] Anne Morrow Lindbergh, "Saint for Our Time,"
The Unicorn and Other Poems (New York: Pantheon Books, Inc., 1956), pp. 45-47.

st. luke
sanctity and medicine

HE FACE of St. Luke is hid from us. A consummate storyteller, he never says "I." A convert, he has kept his conversion high mystery. An Evangelist, he has sketched in ink the heart of Christ, but not his own. A missionary, he has revealed the mind of Paul, but not his own. A doctor who must have treated Paul in his affliction, he has told us nothing of his practice, nothing of his patients, nothing of his methods, nothing of his success. An octogenarian, his eighty-fourth year is as dark as his first.

A "life" of St. Luke, therefore, would be at best splendid fiction. Happily, however, for each physician, there is a pertinent expression in St. Paul's Letter to the Colossians, an expression that will serve as springboard for a series of ideas, ideas that link Luke to the medical man of today. Paul calls

Luke "the beloved physician" (Col 4:14). That expression, "the beloved physician," is the burden of my remarks here.

On broad lines, what is true of most professions is true of medicine: there are three ways of practicing it. Medicine can be slavery; medicine can be an art; medicine can be a vocation.

In the first place, medicine can be sheer slavery. I mean slavery in its strict dictionary sense: what Funk & Wagnalls defines as "involuntary servitude; complete subjection; mental, moral, or spiritual bondage; slavish toil; drudgery." You put in your time, but the hours are riddled with resentment. You resent the unexpected: the ring that wakes you from slumber or the call that takes you from golf. You resent the expected: the office hours and the endless prescriptions, the unspoken fear and the unvoiced plea. You resent the routine, the monotonous: the common cold and the muscular ache, the patient with no symptoms and the patient with all the symptoms. And even where there is no resentment, there is something fearsome: there is no feeling at all. You do your work, and perhaps you do it well; but the heart has gone out of it, the enthusiasm, the thrill. It is just another job. The miracle of birth is swallowed up in blood, and death has become commonplace.

Slavery is not a young man's disease; it commonly comes with time, with age. It is a rut, and a rut is not limited to medicine. It is a peril for priest as well as physician; it is a danger for teacher and lawyer and businessman, for husband and wife; it is a trap for any human being whose task it is to think the same thoughts, to speak the same words, to do the same things over and over again. The slavery is not so much what you do as why you do it; the rut is not the act but the attitude; the drudgery is not in your hand but in your heart.

The curse of such slavery is the curse of all slavery: it is not quite human. You are chained to a wheel. Your mind is not totally given to it, and your will is in rebellion against it.

In the second place, medicine can be an art—a healing art. I mean the skilful, systematic application of scientific truth to the prevention, the cure, or the alleviation of disease. I mean that you can and you should be profoundly dedicated to an absorbing purpose: to bring health to the human person. In its fullness this dedication involves a remarkable wedding of science and art, of knowledge and its use. It involves

131

science—your mastery of a prodigious mass of medical truth, a ceaseless effort to keep abreast of research, in the face of countless new facts, new theories, new procedures, new drugs, in the face of nine hundred American medical journals. This aspect of your art—better, this background for your art—is suggested in a striking sentence in A. J. Cronin's *The Green Years*, where young Robert Shannon, doctor in embryo, says of Dr. Galbraith: "I then perceived his interest to be purely scientific: that strange, beautiful, and wholly disinterested emotion which had already stirred me as I sat at my microscope and which in later years was to afford me some of the rarest joys of my life." [1]

But for the healing art, pure science is not enough; for the application of medical truth, disinterested emotion is inadequate. For, as a physician, you have a perilous, exciting task: to touch science to a person. Not to a body, but to a human being. This demands a rare welding of hand and heart, of professional skill and a warm compassion born of profound understanding. You will see what I mean if you open a 1959 issue of *Life* Magazine. There *Life's* science editor began a series entitled *You and*

[1] A. J. Cronin, *The Green Years* (Boston: Little, Brown & Co., 1944), p. 128.

132

Your Doctor. The opening article of the series was headed: "RX: For Modern Medicine: Some Sympathy Added to Science." The very first paragraph is splendidly pertinent here:

"Of all human acts, few can match the quiet splendor of the moment when the pale and tremulous fingers of a sick person are grasped in the firm, reassuring hands of a compassionate physician. This simple act, mutely promising that all the powers of modern science and human thought will be unsparingly invoked to restore health, is among the finest deeds of humankind. It is more than ritual. When pain and fear make a sick person feel that all is lost, the laying-on of healing hands brings solace and hope. Its strength can even turn the tide of illness and amplify the curative effect of the strongest wonder drug. It remains today, as it has always been, man's oldest medical miracle." [2]

If the curse of slavery is that it is not quite human, the blessing of the healing art is that it is admirably human. The whole man—not merely the mind but will as well, not simply hand but heart too—is put at the service not of a misty mass called humanity, but at the

[2] Warren R. Young, "RX: For Modern Medicine: Some Sympathy Added to Science," *Life*, XLVII (Oct. 12, 1959), 145.

service of a warm, throbbing, hopeful, fearful human person.

But if the healing art is admirably human, it is still imperfect. It is human, yes; and so it is good. But it is not yet divine, and so it is imperfect. There is a third way of practicing your profession; it includes the second, but lifts it to the level of the divine. I mean, medicine can be a Christian vocation. For that, two things are imperative: a realization and a motive. The realization is this: "the laying-on of healing hands" is not just good medicine; it can be authentic spirituality, genuine holiness. For the healing art is your role, your function, in the Body of Christ; it is the specific way in which you reproduce the life of Christ.

Your model in medicine is the healer Christ whom the physician Luke describes over and over again. The Christ who "laid His hand upon each" of the sick "and cured them" (Lk 4:40). The Christ who saw Peter's mother-in-law "suffering from a great fever. And He touched her hand, and the fever left her" (Lk 4:38; Mt 8:15). The Christ who found "a man full of leprosy . . . and stretching forth His hand He touched him, saying: '. . . be thou made clean!'" (Lk 5:12-13). The Christ who "laid His hands" on a woman horribly bent over, "and instantly she was made straight and glorified God" (Lk 13:11-13). You share the work of the twelve apostles whom Christ sent forth not only "to preach the kingdom of God" but also "to heal the sick" (Lk 9:2); you share the task of the seventy-two disciples whom Christ "sent forth two by two before Him" with the command: "Whatever town you enter, and they receive you, . . . cure the sick who are there" (Lk 10:1, 8-9).

The healing art is a share in the life of Christ. But if your art is to lift *you* to the level of the divine, you need a motive—a motive beyond the human, beyond philanthropy and humanity, beyond mere mercy and the milk of human kindness. If your very Christian art is to make you more Christian, you must do this thing which Christ did with a twin motive: you must do it because you love God above all things, and you must do it because you love every human being as the image of God on earth.

One illustration—a twentieth-century Luke: Dr. Thomas A. Dooley III. Tom Dooley was remarkable on several counts. He was remarkable because he consecrated his healing hands and his compassionate heart to a jungle. His practice? The tiny kingdom of Laos in

Indochina. His hospital? Twenty-five
or thirty mats. His assistants? At one
point, two Texas technicians and seventeen Laotian trainees who came to walk
like Texans. His sick calls? The jungles,
and a hundred or more tribesmen a
day. His daily enemies? Typhoid and
tuberculosis, smallpox and leprosy, mal-
nutrition and malaria, beriberi and
anemia, poverty and pestilence.

Tom Dooley was remarkable because
he originated MEDICO, a heart-to-
heart program to bring mercy medicine
to backward areas the world over.
MEDICO helped support not only
Dooley in Laos, but Schweitzer in
Africa, Seagraves in Burma, an eye-
surgery team in India, surgical teams in
Jordan and Vietnam. It had no foundation to finance it, no government grant;
it had only Tom Dooley begging for
men and money and medicine, only the
little people with their nickels and
dimes, like the school for blind children
in Bangkok that sent him seven dollars
each month.

Two and a half years in Laos and Tom
Dooley was more remarkable still; for
at thirty-two he had cancer, black cancer, malignant melanoma. When it was
diagnosed and he recalled the pessimis-
tic statistics on survival, he wrote: "I
knew I was not going to abandon what

I think is the correct thing to do in life because of shadows on a page. Nor was I going to quit this living, loving passion for life that I possess simply because of a statistic. I was not abandoning the beauty and tenderness that man can give to man, just for a statistic." [3]

On the last morning of a world-wide prayer crusade for his recovery, Tom Dooley hobbled into St. Patrick's Cathedral in New York in time for Mass. An ugly hole in his chest was covered by strips of skin from his leg. But at a press conference in Los Angeles he said little of his pain, nothing of the death that loomed ahead. He spoke of two things. He said first: "God has been good to me. He has given me the most hideous, painful cancer at an extremely early age. It's a gift. He wants me to use it. Thousands of people know me. They follow me in what I do. Now I have cancer. That's not important. It's how I react to cancer. These people will see how I react. Thousands of women who have tiny cancers think they can't do the dishes, can't have children, can't go on. As a doctor I know this. Maybe they will say: 'Well, Tom Dooley is

[3] In Agnes W. Dooley, *Promises to Keep: The Life of Doctor Thomas A. Dooley* (New York: Signet Books; New American Library, 1964), pp. 153-54.

137

going back to the stinking jungle. Maybe I can do the dishes.' That is my new gift."

And second, Tom Dooley spoke of his plans. He would return to Laos and his hospital. In the meantime? "In the next six weeks I have to give forty-eight speeches in thirty-seven cities." With the proceeds "I can take care of 72,000 people, including a thousand major surgical procedures." What would keep him going? "It's what has always kept me going: the luck of the Irish, the grace of God, and a little sweat." On Christmas Day, 1959, his plane landed in Laos. On January 18, 1961, he died—thirty-four years old—in Memorial Hospital, New York, a few moments after a priest murmured in his ear: "Son, go now and meet your God."

I am not asking you to give your life to Laos; I am not asking you to pray for cancer. But I am asking you to use your hands and your heart as Tom Dooley used them—because you love God above all else, and because you love each trembling, pain-racked, disease-ridden human being as the image of God on earth. I am asking you to test in your lives the truth of the words that Albert Schweitzer wrote to Tom Dooley: "I do not know what your destiny will be, but this I do know. You will always have happiness if you seek and find *how to serve."* [4]

Medicine can be sheer slavery, or a healing art, or a Christian vocation. If you are a slave, you will deserve to be pitied. If you are a skilled artist, you will deserve to be admired. If you are a consecrated Christian, you will deserve to be loved—loved by men and loved by God. . . . *The beloved physician.*

[4] *Ibid.,* p. 138.

st. francis xavier

sanctity and frustration

WHEN WE think of Francis Xavier, we are tempted to picture a shooting star blazing across the Indian sky, a giant in seven-league boots straddling the Indies and Japan, a conquering hero planting a cross on China's Christless coast. We see "a saint in a hurry," moving seventy-five thousand miles in ten years, much of it on his own bare feet. We see the waters of baptism flowing from his hand ten thousand times in a single month: on a twelve-hour day, one baptism every two minutes for thirty days. We watch him dining with head-hunters, crashing Buddhist monasteries, telling the rulers of Japan: your vices make you "filthier than pigs and much lower than dogs." We see him touch a lifeless boy to life, call a rotting corpse from the earth, stop a funeral procession to give a young man back to his mother.

141

That is the way you and I see Xavier; it is not the way Xavier saw himself. If ever a man felt himself a failure, if ever a human being felt the exquisite agony of frustration, that man was Francis Xavier.

Here is a brilliant mind that has given up the praise of men for love of God. Here is a soul on fire for souls, sent by King and Pope to Portugal's new empire in India. He sets sail, dreaming of countries white for the harvest, of kings and people hungry for the religion of the beloved Portuguese. He reaches Goa, and before his eyes stretches the slave market. Here human beings are paraded like beasts, sold for silver, beaten with whips while their Christian masters, men of Xavier's own race, men of Xavier's own faith, count the blows on their rosary beads!

Men of his own race and faith. They are living in open sin; their god is gold and their own bellies. They will help Xavier, of course—if it does not interfere with their precious traffic. And so Christ is sold for cloves and pepper. No wonder Francis will write to King John of Portugal these strong words: ". . . It is a sort of martyrdom to have patience and watch being destroyed what one has built up with so much labor. . . . Ex-

perience has taught me that Your High-
ness has no power in India to spread
the faith of Christ, while you have power
to take away and enjoy all the country's
temporal riches. . . . It will be a novel
thing . . . to see yourself at the hour
of death dispossessed of your kingdoms
and seignories, and entering into others
where you may have the new experience, which God avert, of being ordered out of paradise." [1]

Xavier turns from his own to the
natives, and his heart sinks. This one
has become a Christian for a new hat;
that one, for a shirt; a third, to escape
hanging. He works wonders among the
peace-loving Paravas, and wild tribes
descend from the hills to slaughter them.
He baptizes six hundred on the Island
of Manar, and a local rajah massacres
them. Never will he see the finish of a
single conquest; never will he repair
the scandal caused by the greedy Portuguese. He cries aloud "his longing to
leave the Indies alone, and to go to
Abyssinia, to Arabia, to Madagascar,
anywhere so that he might do some little
good before he died, for all he had done

[1] *Monumenta Xaveriana* 1, 509-12; translation in
James Brodrick, S.J., *The Origin of the Jesuits*
(New York: Longmans, Green & Co., Inc., 1940),
pp. 133-34.

so far had apparently been brought to nothing." [2]

He opens a second front, in Japan, and the way of the cross starts all over again. If he ever had the gift of tongues, it deserts him now, and he stands, in his own words, "like a statue" amid the chattering crowd. He gives a year of his life to Kagoshima, nets one hundred souls, and its ruler forbids him to preach Christ under threat of death. The nobles insult him till his face turns scarlet; innkeepers shut the door in his face; the common people guffaw at his accent, pelt him with stones. And he writes perhaps the saddest sentence he ever wrote: "The children ran after us with shouts of derision." [3]

He visions a third front: China. He plans his attack with extreme care, and the Governor of Malacca, a Catholic, ruins his strategy. He laughs at excommunication; he calls Xavier "a depraved and vicious hypocrite"; he organizes persecution—and Francis dares not show his face in the streets. "Never in my life have I endured persecution like this, not even from pagans and Mohammedans." And when he leaves Malacca, he leaves

[2] Alban Goodier, S.J., *Saints for Sinners* (New York: Sheed & Ward, 1948), p. 80.

[3] *Monumenta Xaveriana* 1, 660; in Brodrick, *op. cit.*, p. 150.

it for a lonely island, six miles from the China of his dreams, to wait for a boat, a brown sail that will never come. And six miles from China he dies, without a last anointing, without the body of his Christ, with no one to whisper over his frail frame: "May angels lead you into paradise."

"It *is* a martyrdom to watch being destroyed what one has built up with so much labor." These are moving words, for they well up from a heart frustrated, from a remarkable figure who felt himself a resounding failure. But they are more than moving, more than a personal confession; they point up a ceaseless situation, for they echo, at some time or other, from every human heart. It is of this that I shall speak, of human frustration: first, the sheer fact; second, the problem born of the fact; third, a Christian solution to the problem.

First then, the sheer fact of human frustration. I do not mean, at the moment, the minor setbacks inseparable from human living: the headache that yields to aspirin, the heartache that surrenders to a smile. I mean, rather, the reverses and frustrations that sear a man's soul and scar his personality, that disrupt his life and impair his relationship to others, that imperil his career and atrophy his ambition, that keep him from fulfilling himself as a human being and a Christian. I mean, therefore, the marriage that has turned from ecstasy to a joyless thing, from perfect oneness to an armed neutrality. I mean the job that eats up half your waking hours and brings only monotony, fatigue, rebellion. I mean the situation that makes a man a second-class citizen, a second-class human being, even a second-class Christian, simply because his skin is black. I mean the lingering illness that withers your body and threatens to shrivel your soul. I mean the living death of loneliness, the conviction that you are alone and unloved, an unsufferable burden to yourself and to others. I mean the frustration of helplessness: the anguish of a mother who, like Mary beneath the cross, can only watch and wait while a dear one suffers and dies. I mean even the frustrations within Catholic living—wherever a good man's enthusiasm is chilled by an impersonal organization, wherever conscience clashes with tradition, wherever education has been reduced to memory and obedience, wherever the wicked prosper and the good are trodden down, wherever God has hid His face and dark night invades the soul. I mean the frustration of every Xavier as his God-centered life is thwarted by evil.

146

And in our age the fact of frustration has been intensified—on every level: science and art, philosophy and religion, business and politics. For this is a paradoxical age. It is an age of unparalleled progress and astonishing anxiety. Never has there been such success, never so much uncertainty. Never such pride in technology, never such fear of the machine. Never so much victory over nature, never such enslavement to things. Never so much promise, so much pressure. Never so many people, so few persons. Never so many Christians, never such insistence that this is a post-Christian age, that Christianity is irrelevant and God is dead.

The sheer fact of frustration is obvious enough. But from the fact a problem is born. There is a psychological problem, of course: the effect of failure on a man's development as a person. How do you fight that feeling of frustration which builds up an ulcer in the body and a corresponding cancer in the soul —that sense of failure which kills enthusiasm and makes a human being bitter as bile, jealous of the laughter in another's eyes? But I would see even this problem in its religious dimensions: the effect of frustration on a man's development as a Christian. And here the problem has three facets; for frus-

147

tration can touch your faith, your hope, and your love. There is a crisis of faith: How is it possible to go on blindly believing in a gracious God, when God's providence is so elusive, when my little world lies in ruins around me? There is a crisis of hope: How dare I look forward with confident expectation of God's help, when my expectations have been shattered, when God's help has not been there? There is, above all, a crisis of love: How can I go on loving—loving God and man—when my love has been rejected, when my love has been rebuffed?

The solution, on Christian lines, is not simple. A first step, a basic premise, to any solution is a seemingly harsh sentence from Scripture, where God is represented as saying:

My thoughts are not your thoughts,
Nor are your ways my ways. . . .
But as the heavens are higher than the earth,
So are my ways higher than your ways,
And my thoughts than your thoughts.
(Is 55:8-9)

This is dreadfully difficult for a human being to accept—even for a Xavier. Just because I am trying to do God's work with every ounce of my being, is no guarantee that my plans will prosper. There is no guarantee that an effective Christian apostle will not be cut down in his prime, no guarantee that fiery eloquence will be more fruitful than silent suffering, life more redemptive than death. There is no guarantee that because you have given yourself totally to a Christian marriage, your oneness will be lasting; that because you have given your child a godly education, he will not turn from God; that because you love God deeply, you will not lose your job, your home, your family, your health; that because you live like Christ, you can avoid dying like Him. There is no guarantee that because you believe, you will not doubt; because you hope, you will not despond; because you love, your love will not grow cold. There is no guarantee that a Xavier will reach China. In this sense there is a Christian frustration, a Christian failure.

The second step to a solution is closely linked to the first: if God's ways are not our ways, it does not follow that our ways are unimportant, useless, fruitless. As the title of a powerful French movie once put it, "God needs men." Not because He is weak, but because He wants it so. There is no Christian seed which does not bear some fruit: no act of faith which does not somewhere fructify, no Christlike love which does not attract Christ's love. There is no suffering offered to God on the paten of my flesh which is not redemptive, does not bring God's life to someone, somewhere.

Only God knows how much Xavier meant for the China he never saw. You do your Christian task as God gives you to see it; the rest, the increase, is in His hands. God still uses what the world calls foolish to shame the wise, still uses what the world calls weak to shame its strength, still uses what the world calls low and insignificant and unreal to nullify its realities, "so that in His presence no human being might have any ground for boasting" (cf. 1 Cor 1:27-29). The blood of Christians, the love of Christians, is always a seed. In this sense there is no Christian frustration, no Christian failure, this side of hell.

At this stage in our solution the Old Testament has a pertinent story. The Jews were rebuilding the walls of Jerusalem. Among the workmen was Nehemiah. His task was small: to build one section of the wall. Four times the enemies of the Jews sent messengers to him: Come down, let's talk about this thing. And four times Nehemiah sent back the selfsame message: "I am doing a great work, and so I cannot come down" (Neh 6:3).

Here is your answer to frustration, as

it was Xavier's answer: "I am doing a great work, and so I cannot come down." Whether he was sitting at a desk as private secretary to Ignatius Loyola, or washing the sores of a leper in Venice, or teaching catechism to an Indian child, or standing like a statue among mocking Japanese, or simply dying six miles from his dreams, Francis never forgot one thing: "I am doing a great work: I am doing God's work." In his every failure, to the very last failure off the coast of China, he was a resounding success. For, as Paul Claudel said of him, "he did what he was told to do—not everything, but all he was able to do." [4]

The third and final step is a paradoxical Christian truth. In all frustration, the challenge to faith can only be met by deeper faith, more expansive faith, a faith that looks beyond my little world to God's plan for all His world. The challenge to hope can only be met by total trust, utter abandonment to God's design for me and mine. The challenge to love can only be met by greater love, by such selfless love as once inspired a famous sonnet long attributed to Francis Xavier. It is not really his,

[4] Paul Claudel, "Saint Francis Xavier," in *Coronal* (New York: Pantheon Books, Inc., 1943), p. 190.

but it is expressive of his love, and,
please God, it will be expressive of *your*
love. This Spanish sonnet loses something in translation, but the basic idea
breaks through:

It is not your promised heaven
That moves me, Lord, to love you.
It is not the fear of hell
That forces me to fear you.

What moves me, Lord, is you, Lord,
Fixed to a cross and mocked.
What moves me is your wounded body,
The insults and your death.

What moves me really is your love, so that
Were there no heaven, I would love you still,
Were there no hell, I would fear you still.
For me to love you, you need nothing give,
For even if I did not hope as indeed I hope,
Even so I would love you as indeed I love.[5]

[5] The original Spanish text may be found in
Brodrick, *op. cit.*, p. 181; the translation is mine.

st. dismas

sanctity and captivity

OWN THROUGH the centuries many legends have grown up around the Good Thief. One of these stories tells us that when Joseph, Mary, and the Infant Jesus stole into Egypt to escape King Herod, they were set on by robbers. Only a young lad saved them from serious harm. He was a son of the robber chief. This lad had already robbed Joseph when he discovered the Infant in Mary's arms. On Jesus' face he saw such dignity, such majesty, that he knew he was looking on something more than human. In an impulsive act of love he put his arms around the Child and said: "Child, if ever you have a chance to show me mercy, remember me then, and do not forget this moment." And, the legend runs, it is this thief who thirty years later was crucified at the right hand of God.

That tale is legend. It is a lovely story, but there is no good reason for believing that it ever happened. More important, there is something we know did happen. We do not know who the Good Thief was; we do not know where he came from; we do not know how he was captured; even his name, Dismas, we have made up. But this we do know. We know, first, that two convicts were crucified with Christ, two thieves—one on His right hand, the other on His left. We know, second, that one thief cursed Christ for keeping him on his cross; the other whispered "Lord, remember me" (Lk 23:42). We know, third, that to one thief the Son of God promised . . . heaven; to the other He said . . . nothing.

Those are the facts—three simple facts. But those simple facts conceal two profound truths: one truth has to do with captivity, the other with freedom. The truth that touches captivity is this: for a Christian, for any human being, it is not enough to be crucified. In the concrete, it is not enough to be eaten by cancer. It is not enough to die of starvation. It is not enough to be brainwashed and turned inside out by Chinese Communists. It is not enough to suffocate in a gas chamber. It is not even enough to die on a cross a few feet from the Son

154

of God. The proof? Two convicts died an arm's length from Christ. One went to heaven; the other may well have been exiled to hell.

What is it, then, that makes the difference, all the difference between heaven and hell, between peace within and a raging resentment, between love and hate, between the Good Thief and the bad? The difference is the most difficult, the most important part of the Our Father. The most important petition in the Our Father is not "Give us this day our daily bread"; it is not even "Forgive us our trespasses, our sins." The most important prayer in the Our Father is "Thy will be done on earth as it is in heaven." Thy will be done. That prayer the Son of God composed. That prayer He prayed in the garden of His agony, when His sweat became as drops of blood reddening the earth, when His soul saddened so intensely that it seemed He must die. He prayed: "Father, if it is possible, let this cup [this crucifixion] pass from me; yet not my will but thine be done" (Mt 26:39; Lk 22:42). That prayer He made the difference between heaven and hell, the time He let us in on a secret: on Judgment Day "many will say to me: 'Lord, Lord, did we not prophesy in your name? Did we not cast out devils in your name? Did we not work many miracles in your name?' And then I will declare to them: 'Away from me, you workers of evil!' " Workers of evil? How can that be? Because "not everyone who says to me, 'Lord, Lord,' shall enter the kingdom of heaven; but he who does the will of my Father in heaven, he shall enter the kingdom of heaven" (Mt 7:21-23).

But why is God's will so important? For one remarkable reason. It is only when I can say to my God: "Whatever you want, I want," it is only then that I can blurt out with Peter the fisherman: "Lord, you know all things; you know that I love you" (Jn 21:17). "Not my will but thine"—this is what makes saints —saints in the strong sense of the word: human beings who have decided that to have God within them is to have everything. This is what separates genuine saints from pious lip-servers, the mature Christian from the rice Christian, the Christian who gives from the Christian who is out to get. It is the only thing that can make cancer, a concentration camp, a prison cell worth anything. It is the central thing that separated Dismas from Gestas, the Good Thief from the bad. Both were bandits; both had Christ at their finger tips; both could talk to God face to face. And yet, one cursed—cursed Christ, cursed his cross: "If you are the Christ, then save yourself, and save us too" (Lk 23:39). Not so Dismas. He did not ask to be taken down from his cross; one thing only he asked: "Lord, remember me when you come into your kingdom" (Lk 23:42).

But what has all this to do with you, prisoners in the Maryland Penitentiary? Do I mean to stand here and say: prison is God's will for you, a cell block is your way to God, your way to happiness, your way to holiness, your way to heaven? Yes—in a very real sense, yes. Now, understand me. I am not saying that you are guilty of a crime; this I do not know. And because I do not know, I shall not ask you to repeat what the Good Thief said to his comrade: "We are suffering justly enough; we are getting no more than we deserve" (Lk 23:41).

This much, however, I do say. *Here you are;* that is a fact. And what God wants of you grows out of that fact. God is not waiting for you outside; God is here. He is as close to you as He was to Dismas—even closer, if you pillow Him on your tongue in Communion. And God's will for you is this: that by your life you will give witness to Christ, speak out for Christ, as courageously as

157

Dismas did in His death. By your life—
here.

The consoling thing is that so many
of you are doing just that. Each time
you bend your knee before the Hidden
God on this altar, you are whispering
to the world "I believe." Each time you
say the Our Father like a man, you are
like another Christ praying in agony:
"*Thy* will be done." Each time you choke
down the blasphemy, the filth, the anger,
the thousand and one words that foul
prison life, you are confessing that there
is a God whose eye is upon you—in love,
and sometimes in sorrow. Each time
you say to sin "I will not serve," you
declare that you are not a slave to any
man; you are a son of God. Do that,
and you will not merely come closer to
God yourself; you will bring others
closer to Him—so many of us on the
outside who will be more like Christ,
the more like Christ *you* are; so many
of us on the outside who depend on you,
because we are one body in Christ. But
you cannot do it alone; you need God.
And so I recommend to you the prayer
of St. Dismas: "Lord, remember me."
God's answer will always be the same:
"You will be with me in paradise" (Lk
23:43); you will be with me in heaven.

So much for captivity. A second truth
touches your freedom. Six years ago,

159

after a Mass here on the feast of St. Dismas, I asked one of the prisoners what in prison life he found hardest to endure. He was a sensible fellow, intelligent, and he answered: "Father, for the most part it's not too bad. They're quite kind to me here; I'm learning a trade; I have friends; I have some time to myself; even the food could be worse. But the one thing I don't have is the one thing I want: I don't have freedom; I'm not free."

If I were to ask you, his fellow prisoners, the same question—what is the most difficult part of prison life?—I suspect your answer would be pretty much the same. You are strong men; some of you are men of iron. Most of this you can take, most of this you can endure. What is difficult to take, difficult to endure, even for a man of iron, is the most important thing of all: you are not free. You do *what* you are told to do; you do it *when* you are told to do it; you do it *where* you are told to do it. From the moment you rise to the moment you lie down again, you do what the State of Maryland wants you to do. You cannot call your life your own. You are not free.

The point I shall make here is this: there is a part of your life that is completely free, a part of your life that no state can take from you, no power can force. In that aspect of everyday living you do as you please; in every waking hour you are as free as president or pope, you are as free as I am. There is a part of your life that no human being can enter, unless you say yes. I mean your mind, your thoughts.

The point is, what I think, what goes on in my mind, is not determined by where I am. Just because I am kneeling in church does not mean that my thoughts are fixed on God. So too for you. The state can put you behind bars for stealing; it cannot compel you to believe that stealing is sin. The state can put you in total darkness; it cannot extinguish the light in your mind. The state can make you *say* "I'm sorry"; it cannot make you *think* it. The state can keep you here for a lifetime; it cannot make you like it. I can talk to you till sundown with all the warmth of my soul; and you—you can lock me out, you can close your mind to every syllable. Why? Because your mind is your own. God *will* not force it, and man *can*not. There is only one way to destroy this freedom—and that would be to destroy *you*.

It is a remarkable gift, this power to know, this power to think. Why can it not be taken from you by force? Because it is one of the qualities that make you a human being, a being somewhat like God. Do you remember the words of the Bible that describe the creation of man? "God made man to His own image; to the image of God He made him; male and female He created them" (Gn 1:27). What does this mean? It means that every human being bears a striking likeness to his Lord. It means that, whoever you are, whatever you have done, you are a person; there is nobody quite like you. It means that, no matter what your blood or your belief, no matter what your skin or your accent, you share two perfections that are God's: you have the power to know, and you have the power to love.

It is your power to know that interests me now. This is where your freedom lies: you are master of your mind; you can think as you please. But the important question is: what are you going to think about? This is the big question, because it separates the big people from the little, the men from the boys, the good from the bad, the wise from the foolish, the smart from the stupid. It all depends on what is going on inside of you, in that mind of yours which nobody else can touch.

On broad lines, there are two ways

162

you can think. You can, if you wish, make all your thinking center around yourself. You can pity yourself for the pitiful situation you are in. You can blame others—mother, father, relatives, friends, enemies, society, a cop, a stoolie —for what they have done to you or have not done. You can hate, with a hatred bitter as bile. You can plot revenge, lick your lips in devilish anticipation of what will happen when you get out. You can think dirty, lustful thoughts, all the more frustrating because you can do so little about them. You can be selfish and foul-tongued and angry; you can be mean and obscene. And all you will achieve is this: you will be small, foolish, ignorant, inhuman, unloved and un- lovable. In closing your mind to truth and beauty and goodness, in locking out everything except your own small self, you will be a tragic figure, for you will be a man without hope. And a human without hope is not quite human; a man without hope is not quite a man.

Or you can do just the opposite. You can fill your mind with what is true, with what is beautiful, with what is good. By reading and thinking, by talk- ing and listening, by working and learn- ing—yes, by praying too—you can open your mind like a ripening bud to reality. Instead of imprisoning your mind in the Maryland Penitentiary, you can let it roam all over the world, from Baltimore Harbor to outer space. You can fill your mind with history, with the story of man and what he has done, because this is *your* story. You can learn to *do* things, to make and create. You can grace your mind with art and music and literature. You can even think about God. At least, do not close your mind to Him, for He loves you very dearly, and He wants so very much to live in you. Do this, and you will achieve a remarkable change, a transformation. You may not look different; even your language may not change awfully much; but you will be a different person. You will be much wiser, much more mature, much more lovable, much more human. Yes, you will be a little more divine, because in opening your mind to truth and beauty and goodness, you will be a little more like the God who *is* Truth, who *is* Beauty, who *is* Goodness.

Do this, and you will be shaping an attractive future. Here, only your mind is free. But if you open it to knowledge, if you open it to God, then when you are completely free, you will use your knowledge and your freedom as they were meant to be used: to know what is true, to love what is good, and to do what is right.

Live like this, and you will die like Dismas—with Christ at your finger tips: "This day you will be with me in paradise."

st. monica
sanctity and motherhood

In the Church's catalogue of saints, mothers are in a minority. Even where a mother *is* a saint, she is more commonly listed as martyr or widow. Martyr: she died for Christ; widow: her husband died before her. Few saints are listed as "St. So-and-so, wife and mother." In point of fact, few saints have been canonized precisely because they *were* heroic wives and mothers.

At the moment, I am not interested in the reason for this rarity. The reasons are many—from man's centuries-old attitude towards woman to the fact that holiness in the home is a hidden thing, does not make the headlines, is not nearly as eye-catching as an executioner's ax against the throat of Cecilia or a lustful blade in the back of Maria Goretti. I am not concerned with reasons; my purpose is to set before you the Christian concep-

167

tion of saintly motherhood. And my approach has three facets. First, I shall sketch a woman who was a saint specifically as wife and mother. Second, I shall indicate how she achieved sanctity in that situation. Third, I shall suggest what her sanctity means for the contemporary wife and mother.

First then, the woman. The ninth book of St. Augustine's *Confessions* is an uncommon document. There a son tells the story of his mother; a saint tells the life of a saint; Augustine tells of Monica.

If you have ever seen a picture of St. Monica, it was surely Scheffer's painting; it was the portrait that Augustine drew for us when he wrote:

"When the day was approaching on which she was to depart this life—a day that You knew though we did not—it came about, as I believe by Your secret arrangement, that she and I stood alone leaning in a window, which looked inwards to the garden within the house where we were staying, at Ostia on the Tiber; for there we were away from everybody, resting for the sea-voyage from the weariness of our long journey by land. There we talked together, she and I alone, in deep joy; and 'forgetting the things that were behind and looking forward to those that were before,' we were discussing in the presence of

168

Truth, which You are, what the eternal life of the saints could be like, 'which eye has not seen nor ear heard, nor has it entered into the heart of man.' But with the mouth of our heart we panted for the high waters of Your fountain, the fountain of the life which is with You: that being sprinkled from that fountain according to our capacity, we might in some sense meditate upon so great a matter.

"And our conversation had brought us to this point, that any pleasure whatsoever of the bodily senses, in any brightness whatsoever of corporeal light, seemed to us not worthy of comparison with the pleasure of that eternal Light, not worthy even of mention. Rising as our love flamed upward towards that Selfsame, we passed in review the various levels of bodily things, up to the heavens themselves, whence sun and moon and stars shine upon this earth. And higher still we soared, thinking in our minds and speaking and marvelling at Your works; and so we came to our own souls, and went beyond them to come at last to that region of richness unending, where You feed Israel forever with the food of truth: and there life is that Wisdom by which all things are made, both the things that have been and the things that are yet to be.

169

But this Wisdom itself is not made: it is as it has ever been, and so it shall be forever; indeed 'has ever been' and 'shall be forever' have no place in it, but it simply is, for it is eternal, whereas 'to have been' and 'to be going to be' are not eternal. And while we were thus talking of His Wisdom and panting for it, with all the effort of our heart we did for one instant attain to touch it; then sighing, and leaving the first fruits of our spirit bound to it, we returned to the sound of our own tongue, in which a word has both beginning and ending. . . ." [1]

There you have the famous Vision of Ostia—mother and son touching the rim of heaven. But that is Monica shortly before her death; that is her foretaste of eternity, not her life in time. The Monica who worked for sanctity, the Monica who is model of mothers, was a Monica more like the average mother, a Monica of gentle joys and profound sorrows.

Monica, you see, had two problems, a twin crucifixion: her husband and her son. Her husband, Patricius, was a pagan. That much was endurable, for faith comes not from man's deserving, but from God's gracious giving. More

[1] St. Augustine, *Confessions* 9, 10; tr. Sheed, *op. cit.*, pp. 199-200.

bitter still, Patricius was a violent man and a passionate man—hotheaded and hotblooded. His temper was frightening, his infidelity saddening. His lust he loosed on others, his fury he unleashed on her. Adultery and anger—such was Monica's cross with her husband.

Her son Augustine was thirty-three before he was baptized. Brought up a Catholic, a believer in Christ, he gave up faith and morals. He gave up the Christ of Bethlehem and Calvary, the Christ born of a woman and dead on a cross. He joined a heretical sect, because it promised him a free philosophy, a knowledge of nature, an answer to evil; and because it freed him from responsibility for sin: "It was not I who sinned; some other nature sinned in me." [2] And he gave up Christian morality. "Arrived at adolescence . . . I sank to the animal in a succession of dark lusts." [3] At seventeen he took a mistress, lived with her for thirteen years, had a son by her.

These were Monica's crosses for more than thirty years: a husband pagan and profligate, a son torn from Christ and from her. But it was precisely in this situation that Monica achieved sanctity. Not by sheer endurance, but by positive

[2] Cf. *Confessions* 5, 10.
[3] *Confessions* 2, 1; tr. Sheed, p. 27.

action. "The unbelieving husband," St. Paul insisted, "is sanctified by the believing wife" (1 Cor 7:14). And so it was with Patricius and Monica. Their son Augustine tells her secret: "She used all her effort to win him to You, preaching You to him by her character, by which You made her beautiful to her husband, respected and loved by him and admirable in his sight." [4] He was unfaithful, yes; but "she bore his acts of unfaithfulness quietly, and never had any jealous scene with her husband about them. She awaited Your mercy upon him, that he might grow chaste through faith in You." [5] He was violent, yet; but "she knew that a woman must not resist a husband in anger, by deed or even by word. Only, when she saw him calm again and quiet, she would take the opportunity to give him an explanation of her actions, if it happened that he had been roused to anger unreasonably. . . . [Her rule: he was master, she was servant. Other wives] often expressed amazement—for they knew how violent a husband she had to live with—that it had never been heard, and there was no mark to show, that Patricius had beaten his wife or that there had been any family quarrel be-

[4] *Confessions* 9, 9; tr. Sheed, p. 197.
[5] *Ibid.*

172

173

tween them for as much as a single day.
And when her friends asked her the
reason, she taught them her rule. Those
who followed it, found it good and
thanked her; those who did not, went
on being bullied and beaten." [6]

The result? Listen to Augustine again:
"The upshot was that towards the very
end of his life she won her husband to
You; and once he was a Christian she
no longer had to complain of the things
she had had to bear with before he was
a Christian." [7]

Monica's son was a still more difficult
proposition. In his regard she made mis-
takes. It was she who put off his baptism, in the belief that later baptism
would have greater effect. It was she
who advised against an early marriage,
for the sake of his career. It was she
who refused him her home, when he
returned home a heretic.

But these were faults of judgment, not
of love. If any one person under God
won Augustine for Christ, it was
Monica. Twenty years she wept for
him—so freely that a bishop promised
her: "As sure as you live, it is impossible that the son of these tears should
be lost." [8] Twenty years she prayed for

[6] *Ibid.*, pp. 197-98.
[7] *Ibid.*, p. 199.
[8] *Confessions* 3, 12; translation mine.

him; in fact, he tells us that "she served [God's] altar without ever missing so much as a day." [9] She pleaded for him with bishops; she left home to be near him. Above all, her life preached Christ to him: she lived Christianity at every moment—intensely yet humanly, austerely yet attractively. And one day she was able to say to him: "Son, one thing there was, for which I desired to remain still a little longer in this life, that I should see you a Catholic Christian before I died. This God has granted me in superabundance, in that I now see you His servant to the contempt of all worldly happiness." [10]

But what has a fourth-century Monica to do with a twentieth-century mother? Three points are pertinent. In the first place, Monica is a living lesson in a timeless truth: in God's plan, a wife and mother is to reach holiness and Him through husband and child. You may remember how St. Paul, when he needed a symbol to express the union of Christ and His Church, a symbol to reveal the intense love, the two-in-one-ness, the incredible interchange between God Incarnate and His mystical body, fastened on the oneness between husband and wife. Wife stands in relation to

[9] *Confessions* 9, 13; tr. Sheed, p. 207.
[10] *Confessions* 9, 10; tr. Sheed, p. 201.

husband as the Church stands to Christ: you are one—two in one flesh. Between you a like love should live—a love that is dauntless and deathless. Your service of him is service of God—and "to serve God," as the saying goes, "is to be a queen." You sanctify him, as he sanctifies you, for each moment of marriage should prolong and perfect that first moment of marriage, that first whispered yes, that instant at the altar when, as ministers of a sacrament, you gave God to him, and he gave God to you. It is a oneness that grows in holiness as wife becomes mother; for ever since Bethlehem every Christian mother is another Mary, because the fruit of her womb is another Christ.

There is no use in your yearning for some extraordinary union with God like Monica's vision at Ostia. If you are not one with God within your home, you are not likely to be one with God when you leave it.

Monica's second lesson: on this earth, oneness with husband and child, like oneness with God, is an imperfect thing. Oh I know, it is the rare mother who, like Monica, has to seek both husband and son in sorrow. It is the rare mother who brings an Augustine to both birth and rebirth. But Monica's experience is a harsh reminder: your oneness with husband and child can hardly escape crucifixion. And the crosses are legion—from drudgery and monotony, through pain and tears, to separation and death. For love, that many-splendored thing, can be a lonely thing. There are depths of a loved one's being which you cannot enter; there are needs in you he may not see.

The answer—a partial answer, of course—is Monica's answer. Remember Augustine's comment? "She preached You to [Patricius] by her character, by which You made her beautiful to her husband, respected and loved by him and admirable in his sight." The test of love is not a three-syllable sentence: "I love you." The way to oneness is not by words. Your oneness with husband and child will be quickened and deepened if they glimpse in you a trace of God, a trace of Christ. I mean, in the concrete, if, like Monica, your silence is not stubbornness but wisdom; if your words are charged with charity, not dipped in acid; if your tears are not for yourself but selflessly for them; if your service of them is not coldly measured by their service to you; if the Sacrifice you offer of Christ in church finds an echo in the sacrifice you make of yourself at home; if, in a word, you can live the counsel of a famous philosopher:

177

"Let this be your glory: always to love more than you are loved."

For every wife and mother who finds no response in husband or child, who finds him indifferent, ungrateful, blind, there ought often be a pointed question: If he is blind, is it because there is so little to see?

Monica's third lesson: perfect oneness, with God and with dear ones, *will* be yours. Her last recorded words are a gem of faith, of hope, of love. Near death in Ostia, far from her native Africa, she was asked: Are you not afraid to leave your body so far from home? Her answer: "Nothing is far from God, and I have no fear that He will not know at the end of the world from what place He is to raise me up." [11] In Monica's last words lies the hope of every Christian mother: the endless day will dawn when every holy family will be one once again—as Patricius and Monica and Augustine are one—as Joseph and Mary and Jesus are one.

[11] *Confessions* 9, 11; tr. Sheed, p. 203.

st. agnes

sanctity and age

EACH JANUARY the Catholic Church honors a martyr called Agnes. A remarkable thing about this remarkable martyr is that we know so little about her. We know nothing of her family. We know nothing of her life. We know almost nothing of her death. Did she die in Diocletian's persecution, in the early years of the fourth century— or was it a half-century before? We are not sure. Was she burned at the stake, or was her head cut off, or was her throat pierced with a sword? We are not sure. Is the story true that a judge condemned her to a house of prostitution, that a young man who looked with lust on her was struck blind on the spot? We are not sure. Even her name is not beyond dispute. These facts alone we know: she was a Roman; she was put to death by the state; she died for her faith and her chastity;

and, most significant of all, when she breathed forth her spirit she was twelve or thirteen years old.

A strange remark, isn't it? The most significant feature of her life is that, when Agnes died, she was twelve or thirteen. Strange, yes; but thrillingly true. If there is anything a human being clings to, it is life. That is the way God made us: body and soul, He fashioned us with a tenacious grip on that delicate, tenuous, subtle thing called life. And the longer a human being lives, the longer he *wants* to live. Even when he has nothing left to live *for*, he lives for life—sheer life. And it is a good thing, this stubborn hold on life. It means that the human race, human life, will go on. It means that a human being can do so much more good for so many more people. It means that a man can change: that Saul can become Paul, that Augustine the sinner can be transformed into Augustine the saint.

It is a good thing, this leechlike clutch on life, this refusal to die. But the point I would stress here is that it is a dangerous thing too. Millions of human beings are convinced, for various reasons, that the supreme sorrow is death, that therefore the supreme joy is life: the longer, the better. As long as I am reasonably alive, all is reason-

ably well with me. I can see, I can hear,
I can move, I can think, I can talk, I
can touch, I can taste. Splendid! I am
alive! And so the world shakes its head
in pity when it hears of little Agnes.
At twelve or thirteen—on the edge of
young womanhood, on the point of
coming alive—Agnes of Rome dies.
What a pity!

But in point of fact, pity for Agnes
is a wasteful thing, for one remarkable
reason. Life, human life, is not to be
judged by years; Christian life is not
counted on an adding machine; sanctity is not synonymous with senility.
This is the burden of my insight into
Agnes, and I shall unfold it in four
stages.

The first stage: you are not genuinely
alive simply because there is life in
you. This powerful insight, that living
is not the same as life, was captured
some years ago in a novel by Gabriel
Fielding. As the review in *Time* Magazine put it: "The title of this exciting
new novel [*In the Time of Greenbloom*]
sounds like an archaic phrase in cele-
bration of spring. But Greenbloom is
a man, not a season. More important,
he is a state of mind. Greenbloom is
awareness, sentience, ceaseless war on
man's most deadly enemy, which is not
cancer or heart disease, but habit—all

181

the routines of thinking, feeling and doing that enable humans to get through life without living it." [1]

You are not genuinely alive simply because there is life in you. Simply because you watch a time clock from nine to five, or a Late Show from eleven to one. Simply because your standard of living is high, your cholesterol low. Simply because you offer the Sacrifice of the Mass each morning, or are perpetually poor and chaste and obedient. Simply because you sit at a desk or dig a ditch, wash diapers or trump aces. Simply because you eat and dance, weep and laugh, curse and bless. Simply because you are going through the motions of living—"all the routines of thinking, feeling and doing that enable humans to get through life without living it."

The point is this: you are not genuinely alive simply because you are not medically dead. What you do must have meaning for you. Whether you do it once or a thousand times, be it dull or exciting, comedy or tragedy, entertainment or crucifixion, what you do must be humanly done—compounded therefore of intelligence and love. There must be understanding in it, and heart. Otherwise ninety years are no better

[1] *Time*, LXIX (June 10, 1957), p. 104.

182

than nine—only longer. Otherwise you *can* be replaced—by another machine.

The second stage: in the Christian scheme of things, understanding and heart are not quite enough. Every dictator from Herod to Hitler has had purpose and passion, has been amazingly alive, whether he has focused on newborn babies in Bethlehem or on aged folk in Dachau. Sinners can be astonishingly alive, especially in their sin: Saul "breathing slaughter" (Acts 9:1) on the road to Damascus; Augustine "in love with love" [2] in semipagan Carthage; every fictional daredevil with the morals of James Bond. Pagans with the virtues of the pagans are often splendidly alive: an artist at his easel, a scholar at his books, a man or woman who thrills to love. Here is life, and not routine; here are mind and heart, purpose and passion. And still it is not enough. For, in the Christian vision, to live is to "know the only true God and Jesus Christ" (Jn 17:3) whom He has sent. To live is to love the one true God and His Christ, to love every human being as the image of God on earth.

But granted this, given this basic oneness with God in mind and heart, a third stage, a third truth, is highly important. If it is true that human life,

[2] St. Augustine, *Confessions* 3, 1.

183

Christian life, is intelligent love, if it
is true that to live perfectly is to love
to perfection, it is equally true that this
is not so much a question of time as of
intensity. One human being who loves
without reserve can crowd into an hour,
into a single act, a degree of living
which another human being does not
achieve in a lifetime. A mother can
compress a lifetime of love—and therefore a lifetime of living—into the look
of love she fastens on her first-born
infant. A husband and wife who give
themselves to one another totally—
body and soul and spirit—can almost
capture eternity in an hour of time. The
examples are legion. The priest whose
heart is aflame when he breathes life
into a lifeless loaf: "This is my body."
The nun who is marvelously alive when
she whispers: "I vow to you, dear God,
poverty, chastity, and obedience: my
goods, my heart, and my will." The
Christian who holds nothing back from
his act of perfect love: "I love you,
Lord, above all things, because you
are . . . you." Above all, a martyr, a
human being who dies for his God, lives
a lifetime all at once, because in a single
act, in a single instant, he accomplishes
absolutely all that his life was given
him for. In that act, in that instant,
he has loved God with his whole heart,

with his whole soul, with his whole mind, and with all his strength.

And so it was with Agnes of Rome. She was twelve or thirteen. In a sense, life had just begun for her. Marriage, family, social life, deep friendships, adult achievement, these were not yet hers; they would never be hers. And yet, her brief life was a lifetime, because into a few brief hours she crowded a whole life's love. What took her life—fire or sword—makes little difference. In reality, nothing *took* her life, as nothing took her love. She *gave* both, gave life and love, with an abandon that has left sixteen centuries breathless: since the fourth century, Agnes has been the most popular, the most inspiring, of the Roman saints. Perhaps all unknowing, the Christian heart senses instinctively that this child, young in years, was old in love. This child lived fully, because she loved completely.

The underlying idea has been magnificently captured in the Old Testament, in the Wisdom of Solomon:

The age that is honorable comes not
    with the passing of time,
Nor can it be measured
    in terms of years.
Rather, count a man grey-haired
    when he is wise,
Ripe of age,
    when his life is stainless.

185

Divine favor, divine love banished him
　　from a life he shared with sinners;
Caught him away,
　　before wickedness could pervert his thoughts,
　　before wrong-doing could allure his heart.
Such witchery evil has,
　　to tarnish honor,
Such alchemy do the roving passions exercise
　　even on minds that are true metal.
With him, early achievement
　　counted for long apprenticeship;
So well the Lord loved him,
　　from a corrupt world He would grant him
　　　　swift release.
The world looks on,
　　uncomprehending;
A hard lesson it is to learn,
　　that God does reward,
　　does pity His chosen friends,
　　does grant His faithful servants deliverance.
Did they know it,
　　the death of the just man,
　　with its promise early achieved,
Is a reproach to the wicked that live yet,
　　unregarded in their late old age.

(Wis 4:8-16)

"The age that is honorable cannot be measured in years." From this a fourth stage follows, a fourth truth—one of the most difficult lessons for a human being to learn. I mean, the supreme importance of the present moment. There is always a tendency to tolerate the routine of the present, with an eye to the rapture of the future; always the instinct to endure today's

186

travail, in hope of tomorrow's ease. I shall never forget a framed sign in a convent chapel. It read: "Priest of God, say this Mass as if it were your first Mass, as if it were your last Mass, as if it were your only Mass." I suggest that somewhat the same thing can be said to each human being each day: "Child of God, live this day as if it were your first day, as if it were your last day, as if it were your only day."

This is so important, even apart from specifically Christian living; for, as a centuries-old *Salutation of the Dawn* puts it:

Listen to the exhortation of the dawn!
  Look to this day!
For it is life, the very life of life.
In its brief course lie all the verities and re-
    alities of your existence:
  The bliss of growth,
  The glory of action,
  The splendor of beauty.
For yesterday is but a dream,
And tomorrow is only a vision;
But today well-lived makes every yesterday a
    dream of happiness,
And every tomorrow a vision of hope.
Look well therefore to this day!
Such is the salutation of the dawn.[3]

Only then will your senses open consistently to the loveliness and the

[3] In John Bartlett, *Familiar Quotations*, 11th ed. (Boston: Little, Brown & Co., 1950), p. 1064.

majesty of God's creation, to the delicacy of a rose or the warmth of the sun, to the thunder of the surf or the whisper of the wind. Only then will you sense without ceasing the image of God in your fellow man, the urgency of his need, the call for your love. Only then will God be never a stranger, but insistently there.

It is the importance of the "now" in Christian living, in the quest for sanctity. Not that each moment should be a frantic search for God and goodness, for holiness in word and in work; that way madness lies. Simply a sensible awareness that God is here and now: in *this* task, in *this* distress, in *this* stranger, in *this* prayer. Simply the unvarying verse with which a priest opens his breviary each day, the command of the Psalmist to the chosen people: "O that today you would hearken to His voice!" (Ps 95[94]:7). Today—for salvation is *now;* sanctity is *now; "now* is the acceptable time" (2 Cor 6:2).

Agnes of Rome reveals without words that age is frightfully important only if you do *not* love God with your whole heart, only if, like most of us, you are holding something from Him. I do not mean that oneness with God is incapable of increase; I am aware that every Christ, like the first Christ, is expected to grow "in grace before God and men" (Lk 2:52); I know that an Antony of Egypt lived for more than a century and was the holier for it. To that extent age is important.

It is rather, as so often, a matter of emphasis, of perspective, of proportion. The point is not that age is hostile to holiness, but that youth is capable of it. Not that routine is undesirable, but that routine must be penetrated by understanding, and understanding warmed by love. Not that growth in love is insignificant for sanctity, but that love can be perfected in a short space. Not that tomorrow can take care of itself, but that today God speaks and today you must respond.

The message of a martyr and the song of the Psalmist is my warm prayer for you: "O that today you would hearken to His voice!" Today. . . .

st. andrew

sanctity and the search for christ

N St. John's Gospel there is a thrilling scene. The place: the east bank of the Jordan. The date: one of the early days in our Lord's public life. The hour: four in the afternoon. At that hour three men stood near the river, deep in conversation. One was John the Baptist; the other two, his disciples. One of the disciples we can guess: John the Evangelist. The other we know: his name was Andrew. As the three stood talking, Jesus of Nazareth walked by. "Look!" the Baptist cried, "look! The Lamb of God!" At these words Andrew and his friend took off after Jesus. As they drew close to Him, Jesus turned; He looked at them, and He asked them: "What do you want of me?" They answered: "Master, where do you live?" Jesus said to them: "Come and see." So they went, they saw where He lived, and the Gospel tells us "they

stayed with Him all the rest of the day"
—perhaps even the night. When they
left Jesus, the first thing Andrew did was
to search out his brother Peter. The
first thing he told Peter was: "We have
found the Christ." And Andrew "brought
Peter to Jesus" (Jn 1:35-42).

That scene on Jordan's banks is symbolic of Advent. Andrew's experience
trumpets three significant facts, three
stages in the life of a Christian, three
stages in his ceaseless quest for sanctity. Each stage is summed up by a
sentence from that scene; and these
three sentences will be the three points
I shall unfold. First, "Master, where
do you live?" Second, "they stayed with
Him all the rest of the day." Third,
"Andrew brought Peter to Jesus."

First: "Master, where do you live?"
Advent is a search for Christ. Not that
you have totally lost Him; you have
not. But your awareness of Christ may
be misty, shadowy, a gossamer thing that
all but vanishes when you try to grasp
it. The presence of Christ may be a
catechism lesson, committed to memory
but never to the mind. Or it may be
clouded by the presence of others who
seem more real. It is so easy for the
voice of Christ to be drowned out by
sheer noise, for His face to be dimmed

in the smoke of business, for His touch to be unfelt in the rough-and-tumble of simply existing.

Where does Christ live? Only with the Father, high above us in heaven? No. He lives, first, in all the world. He is everywhere, in every nook and cranny of His universe. He *has* to be, because He is God the Son. Look up—at the sun or the stars or the northern lights; He is there. Look down—into the hollows of the earth; He is there. Look out—at the Atlantic billowing to the shore; He is there. Look about you—wherever your eye falls, He is there. He *is* everywhere because He is *active* everywhere, because without Him the sun could not shine nor the snowflake fall; without Him the grass could not grow nor the seas surge; without Him the skylark could not sing, the panther prowl, the shad ascend the rivers.

Where does Christ live? He lives, secondly, in each church building, in the tabernacle. It is true, I do not see Him as Mary did, bundled in straw. I do not reach for Him as Peter did, walking on the waters. I do not speak to Him as Dismas did, bleeding on the wood. I do not grasp Him as Magdalene did, risen from the rock. I do not see the smile part His lips; I do not hear

the music of His voice; I do not trace
His wounds with my finger. But I know
He is there: the same body that once
walked the roads of Galilee; the same
soul that of old grew sorrowful unto
death; the God who is the same yesterday, today, and forever. A hidden
Christ, yes; for He hides His face from
me. But He is there.

Where does Christ live? He lives,
thirdly, within you. To begin with, I
am thinking of the sacred moment when
the Christ you have offered in the Calvary of the Mass gives Himself to you
as sacramental food. I have in mind
Holy Communion: communion because
it is "union with," holy because it is
union with your God.

But this sacramental presence of
Christ serves a further purpose. "My
flesh is food indeed, and my blood is
drink indeed. He who eats my flesh and
drinks my blood *abides* in me and I in
Him" (Jn 6:56-57). Holy Communion
presupposes that our Lord already
lives in you, because you already
love Him. "If anyone love me," the
Son of God declared in the hush of
the Supper Room, "my Father will love
him, and we will come to him and make
our home with him" (Jn 14:23). Holy
Communion is intended to intensify
that abiding presence of God which
began with your baptism and should

195

reach its climax and perfection in endless, ecstatic vision.

Here is Christ's primary advent: His coming to you. Here is Christmas at its most meaningful: the birth of Christ in your inmost being. For the presence of Christ in a stable was only a prelude to the presence of Christ in a soul, to the presence of Christ in *your* soul.

Where, then, does Christ live? He lives in this enormous universe and He lives in a tiny tabernacle. He lives in your body and He lives in your soul. If on Christmas Day, when angels herald His birth, you do not find Him here—in your world, in your church, in your body, in your soul—do not look for Him in the crib. You will not find Him there.

The second significant fact, the second significant sentence: Andrew and John "stayed with Jesus all the rest of the day." Advent is a beginning—nothing more. Once you have seen where Christ lives, then, like the bride in the Song of Songs, never let Him go. There is no reason why the universe should ever stop speaking to you of God, of Christ. There is no reason why a rose should not ravish you as it ravished Teresa of Avila, why the heavens should not enthrall you as they enthralled Ignatius of Loyola. For, as the poet Gerard Manley Hopkins saw, "The world is charged with the grandeur of God." And even if "all . . . wears man's smudge and shares man's smell,"

. . . for all this, nature is never spent;
  There lives the dearest freshness deep down
    things . . .
Because the Holy Ghost over the bent
  World broods with warm breast and with
    ah! bright wings.[1]

If your church, your tabernacle, is a stranger to you save on Sunday, it may well be that you have not really found Christ here, that for you the Real Presence is an unreal phrase, that the sanctuary lamp is a superstition and not a symbol, that you have not learned to sing with St. Thomas Aquinas:

Godhead here in hiding, whom I do adore
Masked by these bare shadows, shape and
    nothing more,
See, Lord, at thy service low lies here a heart
Lost, all lost in wonder at the God thou art.[2]

Is Communion an annual rite for you, and little more? Quite clearly, this kind of ritual cannot satisfy

[1] Gerard Manley Hopkins, "God's Grandeur," in *Poems of Gerard Manley Hopkins,* 2nd ed., Robert Bridges, ed. (London: Oxford University Press, 1930), p. 26.
[2] From the translation of the "Adoro te" by Gerard Manley Hopkins, "S. Thomae Aquinatis Rhythmus ad SS. Sacramentum," *ibid.,* p. 152.

197

a friend of Christ, sate his yearning for God's love. For many of you,
Communion can be a daily union, if
only you will it—better still, if only
you understand it. Understanding will
demand union, and union will deepen
understanding.

All-important is this: once you have
housed Christ in your soul through
love, you can house Him forever. Not,
as with passing friends, for a moment
sadly relinquished; not, as with Andrew,
from four in the afternoon till dawn
breaks the spell; but as long as you
will. For if only God can *give* Himself
to you, only you can *lose* Him.

The third significant fact, the third
significant sentence: "Andrew brought
Peter to Jesus." For a Christian, it is
not enough to have found where Christ
lives; it is not quite enough to stay with
Him all the rest of your days. Your
Christian task is an apostle's task, it is
Andrew's task: to bring others to Christ,
Christ to others. Andrew did it by bringing Christ to what is now Russia and
Turkey and Greece; you must do it by
bringing Christ to your home and your
work and your play. Andrew did it by
dying for Christ; you must do it by
living for Christ—for the Christ who
lives in you. Not by heated argument,
but by intelligent faith; not by arro-

gance or presumption, but by a calm
Christian confidence; not by segregation from those who are different, but
by a love large enough to embrace all
that is human. Such faith, such hope,
such love will bear better witness than
words that you "have found the Christ."

This—all your life long—this must be
your Christmas giving: to share with
others the Christmas gift that has been
given to you. "There has been born to
you a Saviour" (Lk 2:11). Bring Him
to birth in another.

st. nicholas
sanctity and the christmas gift

N THE United States the symbol of Christmas is Santa Claus. Without him an American Christmas is unthinkable. The smallest town possesses him, and the largest city. From New York's department stores to the Santa Claus Post Office in Indiana, *he* is the center of attraction:

He is dressed all in fur, from his head to his
  foot,
And his clothes are all tarnished with ashes
  and soot.
A bundle of toys he has flung on his back,
And he looks like a peddler just opening his
  pack.
His eyes—how they twinkle! his dimples how
  merry!
His cheeks are like roses, his nose like a
  cherry!
His droll little mouth is drawn up like a bow,
And the beard of his chin is as white as the
  snow.
The stump of a pipe he holds tight in his
  teeth,

And the smoke it encircles his head like a
wreath.
He has a broad face and a round little belly,
That shakes when he laughs, like a bowlful of
jelly.[1]

For the average American, *that* is "the
night before Christmas," *that* is the
Christmas spirit. Christmas is Santa
Claus, for Santa Claus is the personifi-
cation of Christmas cheer, the incarnation of Christmas giving.

Do not misunderstand me—I come
neither to bury Santa nor to praise him.
My purpose is more profound: I want
to remind you who Santa Claus really
is, and I want to suggest what his genuine significance is.

First, who is Santa Claus? Santa Claus
came to the American colonies with
the Dutch. More accurately, Santa
Claus is a colonial corruption. What
the Dutch brought to America was not
a figure of fiction but a fourth-century
Christian bishop. The Dutch brought
to the New World a saint from the Old,
one of the most popular saints in the
Christian calendar. They brought to the
New World the patron of Russia and
Greece, of Sicily and Lorraine, of cities

[1] Clement Clarke Moore, "A Visit from St.
Nicholas," in *An American Anthology, 1787–1900*
(Boston–New York–Chicago: Houghton Mifflin
Company, c. 1900), pp. 15-16. For the purposes of
my presentation I have changed all the verbs from
past to present tense.

in Austria and Germany, in Holland and Switzerland and Italy. They brought to the New World the saint of sailors and travelers, the saint of bakers and merchants, the saint especially of little children. They brought St. Nicholas. But in the colonies Nicholas became Claus, and the saint became a jolly old man, bubbling over with all manner of good cheer.

The Old World is here more realistic —and so, more Christian. For much of Europe, December sixth, the date of Nicholas' death, is a holiday, a "holy" day. In Germany, in Switzerland, in Holland, in Belgium, children still receive a "visit" from St. Nicholas on the eve of his feast. A man with flowing white beard, in the robes of a bishop, with miter and crozier, comes to the home as a messenger from heaven. It is the outset of Advent, and so he tells the little ones to ready their hearts for the coming of Christ; he probes them on their prayers; he urges them to be good. And before he walks out into the night, he gives them fruit and candy; for the Nicholas of legend is a saint whose hands were never empty, whose hands were ever open.

So then, Santa Claus is actually St. Nicholas. Then why the indignation? Why contrast the two—the jolly old fellow and the pious old saint? Because, on American soil, Santa Claus has lost something precious. He is still a remarkable figure, admirable, lovable, delightful. But he has lost something: his garments are no longer a vestment; he has ceased to be a symbol of the sacred. Whereas the saint—why, St. Nicholas fairly shouts what the Christmas gift really is, and in so doing he gives us a deep reason for Christmas joy and a Christian basis for our own Christmas giving. This is his genuine significance.

St. Nicholas fairly shouts what the Christmas gift really is. His very presence in chasuble and miter and crozier, his exhortation to prepare by prayer, his plea for goodness in each heart, all these proclaim that Christmas is something sacred, that man *and God* are involved, that the basic Christmas gift is not a gift from man to man, not even a gift from man to God; the basic Christmas gift is a gift of God to man.

That Christmas gift is summed up in a gladsome cry from St. John: "God so loved the world that He gave His only Son, that those who believe in Him may not perish but may have life everlasting" (Jn 3:16). The Christmas gift is God's Son, Christ our Lord. And the captivating words in that sentence are . . . "loved" and "gave."

You see, when man sinned in Adam, man turned his back on Love. With no claim on God's love, he had nevertheless been created in love, had even responded to love. But at the moment of his sin, the man with whom "the Lord God walked" (Gn 3:8) refused to walk with God. At that instant "one man's disobedience made the mass of mankind sinners" (Rom 5:19), severed humanity from divinity. Alive, man was lifeless; still loved by God, he was loveless. Such was human nature at the disastrous moment when the first human being sinned. It was a fearful world, because it had said no to love; a world at enmity with God, because it had rejected God: "I will not serve." It was the world St. Paul described when he wrote four blunt words: "we were God's enemies" (Rom 5:10).

That is why Christmas is so remarkable a gift. The gift would be remarkable enough if God, looking on sinful man, saw hands reaching out in an appeal of love, saw somewhere some tiny spark in human living that called for divine loving. But there was nothing like that at all, no claim at all on love once sin had entered in. And so St. John does not mean that God first saw something that He "loved" in man and then "gave" His only Son. No, John is saying in effect: "God loved the world with an incredible love; I mean, He gave His only Son." As John phrased it in a letter: "In this has the love of God been shown in our case, that God has sent His only Son into the world that we may live through Him. The love consists in this, not that we have loved God, but that He has first loved us: He sent His Son as an atoning sacrifice for our sins" (1 Jn 4:9-10). God's love for the world *is* the gift of His Son. In His giving is His love. To love is to give.

The Christmas gift, then, is astonishing for two reasons. In the first place, because it is sheer gift. I had no claim on God's love, no right to His gift. He gave because He is Goodness, because He wanted to give. In the second place, *what* God gave was astonishing. Not an angel like Gabriel; not a prophet like Isaiah; not a king like David. God gave His own Son. And He gave Him not in vision in a burning bush, but in person in a feeding trough. He gave not a God who was far from man's touch, but a God-man who shook with cold, winced at insult, wept over a grave, sweat blood from fear, and died in agony. And dying in agony He gave

God back to the man who had lost Him.

Precisely there is the incredible perfection of the Christmas gift. God did not say: "Here is my Son. Now you see Him come in a stable of earth to save the world; centuries hence you will see Him coming on the clouds of heaven to judge the living and the dead." No; the perfection of Christmas is that Christ is not a past event or a future prediction. He is a present reality. He came primarily to rest not in straw or on clouds but in souls. What man had lost, God gave back to man. The only gift that can bring man back to God, God gave to man, God gives to man. God gives man. . . God.

This, then, is the Christmas gift: God within you. This *is* God's love. And with God within you, you have a deep reason for Christmas joy. In the Introit that opens the Mass for the Second Sunday of Advent, the Church borrows a sentence from the prophet Isaiah and chants it to the Christian people as they long for Christmas: "People of Sion, look! The Lord shall come to save the nations; and the Lord shall make the glory of His voice heard in the joy of your heart." Joy is a sign of God's coming, and God's coming brings joy—joy in the realization that the redemption which touched the world on a blessed night lodges in your soul these blessed days, that in your sinlessness God lives in you, God loves you.

And finally, God's gift of Himself gives a Christian basis for your own Christmas giving. The perfection of your Christmas giving, of course, is to give yourself totally to Christ, to return love for love. If God is within you, such a gift is entirely possible. A second striking gift is to give someone else to Christ, to bring Christ to birth in another—in one who has never had Him, or in one who has had Him but has lost Him. But even your lesser gifts—the Gillette or the Corvette, the Marlboro or the Paper Mate—even your lesser gifts will take on Christian meaning, the more closely they resemble the first Christmas gift, the more selfless you are and the less calculating, the more your gift stands for you, the more the gift is love and love is the gift.

I would urge on all of you what a German philosopher urged on woman alone: "Let this be your glory: always to love more than you are loved."

st. lucy
sanctity and light

FOR DIFFERENT people, St. Lucy is different things. For the historian, Lucy is a saint of Sicily who was put to death in the persecution of Diocletian, December 13, 304. For the gondoliers of Venice, Lucy is their patron and protector, and the haunting song "Santa Lucia" flows affectionately from their lips as they sweep majestically through the canals. But for the Christian people down the ages, Lucy has been linked with light. Light is what her name means. And so, centuries ago, she became the saint to invoke for the light of the body—I mean, in diseases of the eyes. For centuries, as long as street lamps were lit by hand, lamplighters had Lucy for patron. Before the calendar reform, her feast fell on the shortest day of the year, and so in Scandinavia Lucy was the "light saint" who broke the tyranny of winter darkness and brought the light to rule once again. In northern Europe Lucy candles burned in the home, Lucy fires in the open. Lucy was the bringer of light: light to the body, light to the world.

And that is precisely Lucy's position, her function, in Advent. She is a symbol, a kind of sanctuary lamp. In mid-Advent the light that is Lucy proclaims Him whom St. John called "the true light, that enlightens every man born into the world" (Jn 1:9). If St. Andrew reminds us that Advent is a *search* for Christ, if St. Nicholas reminds us that the basic Christmas *gift* is Christ, St. Lucy reminds us that this same Christ is the *light* of the world.

The problem is, it is hard to think of our Lord as light. It is easy enough to see Him as a baby rustling in straw; as a carpenter planing a tree; as a healer cleansing a leper; as a teacher charming the Temple; as a convict bleeding on a cross; even as risen from the grave and munching fish on a lake shore. But to think of Him as light—this passes understanding. It may be poetry; it is not reality.

But the fact is, this *is* reality. Zachary saw it six months before the birth of Christ. Filled with the Holy Spirit, he prophesied in awe: "Such is the merciful kindness of our God, which has bidden Him come to us, like a dawning from on high, to give light to those who live in darkness, in the shadow of death" (Lk 1:78-79). Simeon saw it six weeks after the birth of Christ. Led by the Holy Spirit, he took the child in his arms: "Now, O Lord, thou dost let thy servant go in peace. . . . This is the light which shall give revelation to the Gentiles" (Lk 2:29-32). Christ Himself proclaimed it thirty years later: "I am the light of the world. He who follows me does not walk in the darkness but will have the light of life" (Jn 8:12).

But what does it mean to say that Christ is the light of the world? It means that redemption touches man's mind, that sinful man was in darkness, and God came to tear away the darkness. How? In the first place, the Son of God came on earth not simply to *do* something, but to *say* something. "This is the light," Simeon said, "which shall give revelation." He was born not only to die; He was born to teach. "This is why I was born," He told Pilate, "this is why I have come into the world: to bear witness to the truth" (Jn 18:37).

And the truth He revealed is a brilliant light for man's mind, because He told us secrets unsuspected about God and about the image of God that is man. He told us about the secret life of

211

God—the life Father, Son, and Holy
Spirit live alone, without ever being
lonely. He told us of a God who, uncompelled, sent His only Son to die in
rare anguish for a race that had rebelled,
a race that cried "I will not serve." He
told of a food that would be His flesh,
of a drink that would be His blood. He
told of a body that would prolong His
presence till time is no more, a Church
that would be Christ teaching, Christ
ruling, Christ sanctifying. He told of a
new life, a life that is God's life throbbing through man's being. He told of
seven symbolic acts which would chan-
nel that life to men: a baptism to begin
it, a confirmation to perfect it, a Eucha-
rist to feed it, a penance to recapture
it, an ordination to communicate it, a
marriage to perpetuate it, a last anointing to link this life to the next. He told
of a life beyond this life, where, as the
Mass for the Dead puts it, "life is not
taken away, life is merely changed";
where man's happiness is God, face to
face, days without end, rapturous and
ecstatic, without pain, without tears.

All this He told us, and a thousand
truths more. This is the light that shattered the darkness one blessed midnight. There was nothing to rival it
before Bethlehem; there has been
nothing to match it since. In the face

of that revelation, man's discovery of the atom pales into insignificance. This is the *God* of the atom speaking to man —not from a bush, not from a cloud, but from human lips; lifting man's mind not to outer space but to God's inner life. No wonder He could say on the eve of His death: "I have called you friends, because all things that I have heard from my Father I have made known to you" (Jn 15:25).

So then, our Lord is the light of the world because He enlightened the world with the secrets of God. But this light is not enough. Christ did not thunder from a mountain, plead from a boat, and whisper from a cross in order that His words might hover in the Judean air, or lie imprisoned in a Bible, or reach man's mind like ancient history. God's revelation calls for a response. If God speaks to man, it is in order that man might speak to God. If Christ proclaims: "Amen, amen, I say to you," it is man's task to answer with the centurion: "I believe, Lord; help my unbelief." If the first light is revelation, the corresponding light is faith.

And faith *is* a light. Because with it your mind, however unlettered, is incredibly unfettered, and without it your mind, however brilliant, is unbelievably dark. With it you can affirm what a

213

Huxley can only deny: that even an evolving universe needs a God. With it you can assert what an Aristotle could never suspect: that God is not only One but Three. With it you can see on a cross not injured innocence but God redeeming; in a small white wafer, not lifeless bread but the Bread of Life. With it you can see God in the water that bathes a baby's brow and in the oil that anoints an old man's lips, in the hand of a priest upraised to forgive and in the words of self-giving that a bride and groom murmur to each other. With it you can see in sorrow joy, in pain redemption, in death unending life. You can do so because in faith you use God's eyes to see, and so in the dark you can know breath-taking truths that only God has a right to see.

This is our Lord's twin gift of light, and it has been given to each of God's people. The first gift was given over nineteen centuries ago, in a little corner of the world; the second gift is given today, in a little corner of your mind. The first gift was God's revelation to you; the second gift is your response to God. Both are gifts, because both are undeserved; each is God's gracious giving. Both are light, because one opens God's mind to you, the other opens your mind to God. It is this twin light

214

that God perfects from day to day, as He broadens your vision of what is true, as He enlightens your mind to see the good that must be done, the evil you must shun. It is a lifelong experience, which will end only when the dim light that is faith gives way to the dazzling light that is vision, and you see face to face the Truth that once huddled in a manger and now hides in your mind.

I am not surprised that in the Mass for the Third Sunday of Advent the Church prays to Christ: "Turn your ear, O Lord, to our petitions, and by the grace of your coming to us bring light to the darkness of our minds." Bring light. . . .

st. thomas the apostle

sanctity and christmas faith

T was the first Easter Sunday. The time: evening. The city: Jerusalem. The group: ten special friends of Jesus. The scene: a supper room, where seventy-two hours before He and they had supped together. The doors of the room were bolted, for the ten were terrified: their leader had been crucified, and the city was seething. Suddenly the same Christ who had passed through the sealed door of Mary's womb, the same Christ who had passed through the sealed door of the tomb, the same Christ passed through the sealed door of the supper room. "Peace!" He said to the ten. "Peace!" And He showed them His pierced hands and the hole in His side.

That evening two of Jesus' special Twelve were not there. One was Judas, the other, Thomas. Judas was not there because he had hanged himself with a

217

halter. Why Thomas was not on hand, we do not know. In any event, when Thomas came, Jesus was gone; and the ten pounced on him: "We have seen the Lord!" "Oh, have you?" Thomas asked. "Unless I see in His hands the print of the nails, unless I put my fingers where the nails were, unless I lay my hand into His side, I will not believe."

One week passed. Came the first Sunday after Easter. The same room, the same friends. But this time, only Judas was absent. Once again the doors were bolted, and once again Jesus passed through. To all He said: "Peace!" To Thomas He said: "Let me have your finger; put it here, and look at my hands. Now let me have your hand; lay it into my side. Cease your doubting, and believe!" In the hush that followed, Thomas murmured: "You are my Lord and my God." Jesus' response was a question: "Because you have seen me, is that why you believe?" (Jn 20:19-29)

Dear friends in Christ: The first Easter takes us back to the first Christmas. The crisis Thomas faced in the supper room is the crisis a Christian faces in the stable. As you look upon the child in the manger, there is an affirmation that should fall from your lips, and there is a question that does fall from His. Your affirmation: "You are my Lord and my God." His question: "Because you have seen me, is that why you believe?" That affirmation and that question will be my two primary ideas in this chapter.

First, your affirmation. Since the crux of Christmas is Christ, Christmas can be any one of three things. Conceivably, Christmas may have *no* relation to Christ, or it may have a *wrong* relation to Him, or it may have the *right* relation.

For some, Christmas has no connection with Christ. For them, the spirit of Christmas is the rollicking song that harks back to seventeenth-century England:

> Now thrice welcome Christmas,
>   Which brings us good cheer,
> Minc'd pies and plum porridge,
>   Good ale and strong beer;
> With pig, goose, and capon,
>   The best that may be,
> So well does the weather
>   And our stomachs agree.

The halls are decked with boughs of holly; an evergreen lights the living room; gifts cover the carpet; but Christ is not there. The Christian carol has been replaced by "A Christmas Carol," St. Luke by Charles Dickens, the Christ child by Tiny Tim. And at best the

219

Christmas refrain is a misty, jolly "God bless us, every one!"

For others, Christmas has a relation to Christ, but it is a wrong relation. At bottom, this means that the child in the straw is just that and nothing more. Oh yes, there is poetry here: a star to light a stable; angels sweetly singing o'er the plain; shepherds hurrying over a hillside; kings on their knees. There is lovely sentiment: we can sing a lullaby to the child:

> Sleep, sleep, my own:
>   Thy mother's arms enfold thee.
> Lo, at thy borning
>   The winds of the morning grow still.
>
> Sleep, sleep, my child:
>   Bright angels behold thee.
> Now all is peace
>   In the cave on the hill.

There is tragedy too: infants put to the sword because they look like Jesus; a flight into exile from the fury of a tyrant. There is even rich promise: this child will flower into a man without peer in power, without equal in love, without rival in sacrifice. This child will lead men back to God. But, when all is said and done, this is a human being and nothing more!

But a Catholic Christmas not only has a relation to Christ; it has the right

221

relation. The authentic Christian concept is captured in the very word "Christmas." Christmas means Christ-Mass, the Mass of Christ. When the word "Christmas" was born nine centuries ago, the whole Christian world confessed that the core of Christmas is the Sacrifice of the Mass.

You see, the purpose of Christmas was Calvary. Christ was born to die. He lay in a crib of clay because one day He was to lie on a cross of wood. The essence of Bethlehem is this: God was preparing a body, His body, for sacrifice. The New Testament Letter to the Hebrews gives the essence of Bethlehem when it says: "At His entrance into the world Christ says [to His Father]: '[The] sacrifice and oblation [prescribed by the Law] you did not wish; but you have fitted together a body for me. In burnt offerings you took no pleasure. Then said I: Here I am; I have come to do your will, O God'" (Heb 10:5-7). Thirty years later the body that had been readied for sacrifice in Bethlehem was ready for sacrifice on Calvary: "This is my body, which is being given for you. This is my blood, which is being shed for you" (Mt 26:26-28; Lk 22:19-20). Crib and cross have one meaning: a God-man offers Himself to God for the sins of man.

222

And in the Sacrifice of the Mass God gives us Calvary all over again. The priest is the same: the God-man. The victim is the same: the God-man. The purpose is the same: to make the children of men children of God. A significant difference: today the God-man offers Himself to God through the lips of men—through your lips and mine. From crib to cross to altar—that is the story of Christmas, because it is the story of the Christ-Mass. In this perspective, isn't it a meaningful thing that the most cherished of Christmas carols, "Silent Night," was first performed at a Midnight Mass? Midnight for Bethlehem; Mass for Calvary. God in a crib, God on a cross, God on an altar. Indeed "you are my Lord and my God."

Your Christmas affirmation, therefore, is the Easter affirmation of St. Thomas: "You are my Lord and my God." There remains only a question—the question the risen Christ put to Thomas: "Because you have seen me, is that why you believe?" For Thomas, the question was a dilemma indeed. He could hardly say no, for he had announced categorically: "Unless I see the print of the nails, I will not believe." It was painful to say yes, for our Lord had added: "Blessed are those who have *not* seen me and yet believe."

But for you, the question is quite simple. "Because you have seen me, is that why you believe?" Your answer is . . . no. On the one hand, you do believe. You believe that this is God in a crib, God on a cross, God on an altar. On the other hand, you have not seen Him. You were not at Mary's side in the stable; you did not stand with Mary beneath the arms of the cross; and the Christ of the Mass is a hidden God.

The point is: seeing is *not* believing. To believe is to accept something as true, not because you see it is so, but because someone who ought to know says it is so. When you kneel at the crib, or on Calvary, or in church, and affirm "This is God in flesh," you affirm it not because you see it is so, but because God says it is so. Oh yes, it is a reasonable affirmation: I can pile proof upon proof, evidence upon evidence, to persuade you that only a world in which Christ is God makes sense out of history. But, in the last analysis, you and I can murmur to Christ, "You are my Lord and my God," not because we have proved it, but because God has revealed it. And how do I know He has revealed it? Because the Light of the world has given even that light to my mind.

A gentle suggestion: do not think too

harshly of Thomas. We do not know whether he actually put his finger into Christ's hand or laid his hand into Christ's side; the Gospel story does not quite say so and the Christian sense feels he did not. But even if he did, even if he tested with his own flesh the reality of Christ's risen flesh, his act of faith still went beyond the evidence. No man can say to Christ, "You are my Lord and my God," on the evidence of his senses or of sheer reason. At that critical moment our Lord could have said to St. Thomas what He said on a similar occasion to St. Peter: "Blessed are you, Simon. . . . It was not flesh and blood that revealed this to you; it was my Father in heaven" (Mt 16:17).

And so, as you whisper "You are my Lord and my God" in Bethlehem, on Calvary, or in your parish church, I say to each of you: "Blessed are you. It was not flesh and blood that revealed this to you; it was your Father in heaven."

st. mary magdalene
sanctity and easter renewal

T was the first Easter. It was very early, St. John says, still dark, when a woman made her way to the tomb of Christ. But the tomb was empty. A shelf in the rock, yes; linen bands that had caressed His body, yes; the handkerchief that had shrouded His face, yes; but no body, no face of Christ. Like a woman possessed, she ran to the city to tell His friends. Two she found, Peter and John, and to them she blurted out an anguished sentence: "They have taken the Lord from the tomb, and we do not know where they have laid Him." Peter and John rushed to the rock, went in, saw that their Lord was no longer there, and returned in wonder to Jerusalem.

Not so the woman. The woman remained at the rock, stood outside the tomb in tears. Even when two angels addressed her, "Why are you weeping?"

the answer was the same anguished sentence: "Because they have taken away my Lord, and I do not know where they have laid Him." Even when a man appeared, a man she took for the gardener, a man who asked as the angels had asked, "Why are you weeping?" the agitated answer was much the same: "Sir, if it was you that removed Him, tell me where . . . and I will take Him away."

In her distress the woman turned once again to the tomb. But at that moment the man spoke again—one soft, revealing word: "Mary." And she turned and spoke in answer—one wild, revealing word: "Master." She fell at His feet, laid hold of them in unrestrained love, tore herself away only at His bidding, only to run to the city and declare to His disciples the message that would change the world: "I have seen the Lord . . ." (Jn 20:1-18).

The woman in that Easter episode is, of course, Mary Magdalene. It is an exciting episode, with many a lesson for the Christian reader: a lesson in love, crucified love, deathless love, risen love. But the reason I have retold this incident is far more basic than any isolated lesson. The life story of Magdalene suggests, in germ, the salvation story of Easter, and the story of Easter reveals, in substance, the life of a Christian. From Magdalene, through Easter, to the contemporary Christian—such is the movement of my thought.

First, what is the life story of Mary Magdalene? What do we know of this uncommon woman, this native of Magdala on the western shore of the Lake of Galilee? What we know of her we know from the Gospels, and from the Gospels we can gather only four facts about her—but each fact is precious. The first fact is a clause from St. Luke: "Mary of Magdala, out of whom seven devils had been driven" (Lk 8:2). An elusive expression, this "seven devils." It need not mean that she was a sinner. But was she not the sinful woman who washed the feet of Jesus with her tears and dried them with her hair, the woman whose many sins were forgiven her because she loved so much? The Gospels do not say. Oh yes, Western Christians down the centuries have thought so, have made Magdalene synonymous with repentant sinner. But the Gospels do not say so, do not suggest that the sinner in the house of Simon was Mary Magdalene. Of Magdalene they tell us that the Lord had driven seven devils from her. Perhaps she did sin much, but "seven devils" do not prove it. She may simply have

229

suffered much—an affliction that racked
her flesh, tortured her nerves, beyond
her body's power to endure. From such
affliction—perhaps rooted in sin, perhaps
not—from such devils Christ delivered
her.

This new-found freedom opened a
new life for Magdalene. For the Gospels reveal a second significant fact in
her life story: once our Lord had healed
her, Mary followed Him. She was one
of a remarkable group of women—
Joanna and Susanna, Salome and the
mother of James the Less—women who
walked with Christ as He preached the
gospel, "waited on Him" (Mk 15:40),
"provided for" Him and the Twelve
"out of their means" (Lk 8:3). Totally
consecrated to Christ and His kingdom, they gave of their time and their
money; they cooked and they washed
and they sewed; they laughed with Him
and wept with Him and prayed with
Him. In a genuine sense, they spread
the gospel—not by word but in work,
not miraculous signs but unremitting
service. Such was Mary Magdalene,
handmaid of Christ, servant of His
servants. Even then she could have confessed: "it is no longer I that live, but
Christ that lives in me" (Gal 2:20).

The third precious fact about Magdalene comes from Calvary, from the

231

pen of an apostle who was there. St. John tells us: "Now there were standing by the cross of Jesus His mother, and His mother's sister, Mary of Cleophas, and Mary Magdalene" (Jn 19:25). A simple sentence on the face of it, but really quite remarkable. While the disciples of Christ cowered elsewhere in fear, while passers-by railed at Him and Roman soldiers cast lots for His garments, while robbers reproached Him and men of God mocked Him, Mary Magdalene stood by the cross of Jesus. It is a striking thing: every time Magdalene is mentioned in the Crucifixion story, the one constant refrain is that she wants to be close to Christ. They nail Him to a cross; she stands beneath the cross. They roll a great stone to the entrance of the tomb; she sits opposite the stone. She must leave Him on Saturday; she returns early Sunday to anoint His body. Even when there is nothing to see but an empty grave, there she stands, by the lifeless rock, in tears because they have taken Him from the tomb and she knows not where they have laid Him. Here is a love that defies death, that deepens with death, a love that asks one thing of love: to be one with Christ, in life and in death.

The fourth precious fact about Mag-

dalene comes from the empty tomb,
from the risen Christ. She has seen Him
live, and she has seen Him die; now
she sees Him gloriously alive. "Mary,"
He murmurs. "Master," she cries. Anguish turns to ecstasy, crucifixion to
resurrection—and Mary Magdalene dis-
appears from the pages of history.

Such is the life story of Magdalene.
But the life story of Magdalene suggests, in germ, the salvation story of
Easter. As with Mary, so here, there are
four stages in the story. The story began,
not with seven devils, but with one. I
mean the hour in Eden when Satan
ruined God's plan for man, when two
human beings had to hide from God
because they no longer loved Him, when
humanity inherited from its father sin
in place of love, concupiscence instead
of continence, death in lieu of life. I
mean those ages upon ages when men
cried out:

Therefore is justice far from us,
And righteousness does not reach us;
We look for light, but lo! darkness,
For the rays of dawn, but we walk in gloom.
We grope like blind men along a wall,
Like men without eyes we grope;
We stumble at noonday as in the twilight,
In the strength of manhood we are like the
    dead.
All of us growl like bears,
And sadly moan like doves;

233

We look for redress, but it comes not,
For salvation, but it remains far from us.
(Is 59:9-11)

The second stage began when salvation came close to us, when God became man to make men gods—the silent, holy night when a virgin bent over her Lord to whisper: "This is my body." With men like Peter and women like Magdalene, this God-man walked the ways of Palestine, announcing an astonishing new order of things: that God had sent His only Son into the world, not to judge it but to save it; that in Him the ageless, breathless longing of men would find fulfilment; that He was life for the lifeless and light for the sightless, bread for the hungry and water for the parched; that in Him had come to birth the prophecy of old:

The Spirit of the Lord is upon me;
    for He has anointed me:
To preach the good news to the poor He has
        sent me,
    to proclaim to the prisoners their release,
    and sight to the blind,
To set at liberty the oppressed. . . .
(Lk 4:18-19)

Through Him, God and man in one, man and God would be one once again. But not by words alone; not by signs and wonders; not by a transfiguration on Thabor. "We are going up to Jeru-

234

salem, and all things that have been written through the prophets concerning the Son of Man will be accomplished. For He will be delivered to the Gentiles, and will be mocked and scourged and spit upon; and after they have scourged Him, they will put Him to death; and on the third day He will rise again" (Lk 18:31-33).

And so the third stage came in the story of salvation: Calvary. For in God's surprising ways, life would return to man through death, life to the sons of men through the death of the Son of God. It is St. Paul's amazed reflection: "When we were still helpless, at the decisive moment Christ died for us godless men. Why, a man will hardly give his life for an upright person, though perhaps for a really good man some may be brave enough to die. But God proves His love for us by the fact that Christ died for us when we were still sinners" (Rom 5:6-8). For us, for every human being—for Adam exiled from Paradise and Cain marked by murder, for a faithless Pharaoh and an adulterous David, for the Pharisee and the publican, for Caiphas and Barabbas and Judas, for Peter and James and John, for Mary of Magdala and Mary of Nazareth, for the last human being who will touch this earth with his sin or his sanctity—for each one the Son of God was lashed and nailed, for each one He bled and died. Each can confess with St. Paul: "He loved me and gave Himself up for me" (Gal 2:20).

But the story of salvation does not end with redeeming death. There is a fourth stage, and it dawned with the first Easter. It is the empty tomb and the stone rolled back; it is the question of angels to frightened women: "Why do you look among the dead for Him who is alive?" (Lk 24:5) A unique event, yes. But the resurrection of Christ is not just a matchless miracle; it is not primarily a page in apologetics, a proof that He is God. No, His resurrection is part and parcel of our redemption. For two remarkable reasons. First, as Paul put it, "Christ has risen from the dead, the first-fruits of those who have fallen asleep" (1 Cor 15:20). In His humanity risen from the grave, humanity itself returns to God. In His sinless flesh, sinful flesh is reconciled to God. Second, as Paul phrased it, by His resurrection "the last Adam has become a life-giving spirit" (1 Cor 15:45). Not that the Son of God has become the Holy Spirit; not that the Second Person of the Trinity has become the Third. Rather that by His resurrection the humanity of Christ passed from one state to another, from

236

the state of earth-bound flesh to a spiritual state, to a state that empowers Him to give life, His life, the life that saturates His humanity, to all men. In a word, the resurrection of Christ is man's return to God and God's return to man. This is the deep meaning of St. Paul's contention to the Corinthians: "If Christ has not risen, your faith is a delusion; you are still in your sins. Yes, and those who have fallen asleep in trust in Christ have perished" (1 Cor 15:17-18).

Such is the salvation story of Easter. But the story of Easter reveals, in substance, the life of a Christian. As with Magdalene, so here; as with Easter, so here: there are four stages. There is a new birth and a new life, there is crucifixion and resurrection.

There is a new birth. At your baptism devils were driven out: "Depart," a minister of Christ commanded, "depart, every unclean spirit, from this creation of God, whom our Lord has graciously called to be a temple of the living God." And once the power of Satan was shattered, the life of God entered in. You were a new creature, splendidly alive, alive with the life of the risen Christ. For, as St. Paul told the Christians of Rome: "Do you not know that all of us who have been bap-

237

tized into Christ Jesus have been baptized into His death? Through baptism
we have been buried with Him in death,
so that just as He was raised from the
dead through the Father's glory, we
too may live a new life" (Rom 6:3-4).

This new life, this Christ life, this
Easter life, you are living now. You live
it each sinless moment, in laughter or
tears, at work or play, silent or eloquent, in your room or on the streets.
You live it with each burst of belief,
each hymn of hope, each look of love.
You live it in your prayer to God and
in your care for men. White or black,
American or Hungarian, young or old,
you live this Easter life as long as you
can say: "It is no longer I that live, but
Christ that lives in me" (Gal 2:20).

But this Christ life, like the life of
Christ, involves crucifixion. For the
death you died to sin in your baptism
calls for a corresponding death to self
each day—increasingly so, as with the
years God strips from you relentlessly
so much that sweetens existence on
earth: health and strength, enthusiasm
and passion, freedom and self-sufficiency, the power and the glory, even
friendship and love. And the day will
dawn when God will ask of you the
ultimate gift of self, will ask that like
the first Christ you too be "obedient

unto death" (Phil 2:8). It is your share in the sacrifice of Christ; it is Magdalene by the cross.

And yet this new life, this Christ life, this crucified life does not die with death. Basic to the Easter story is the thrilling promise of Christ: "I live, and you shall live" (Jn 14:19). That promise is the Christian affirmation that leaps at us from the Preface of each Mass for the dead: "For those who believe, Lord, life is not taken away, life is merely changed." Not simply in soul, but finally in body as well—what Paul revealed to the Christians of Corinth: "I will tell you a secret: . . . we shall all be changed, in a moment, in the twinkling of an eye. . . . For the trumpet will sound, and the dead will be raised free from decay. . . . And when this mortal nature puts on immortality, then what the Scripture says will come true: 'Death has been triumphantly destroyed. Where, death, is your victory? Where, death, is your sting?' " (1 Cor 15:51-55) Then shall the risen Christ murmur your name as He murmured Magdalene's: "Mary." Then shall you turn to Him, turn to Him eternally: "Master." Then shall the risen Christ and the risen Christian be one, in a ceaseless, ecstatic Easter.